"THE BEAST"

by

Dr. Leland Jensen

Knight of Baha'u'llah,
Establisher of the Baha'i Faith

*"The Most Great Law is come, and
the Ancient Beauty ruleth upon* **the throne of
David.** *Thus hath My Pen spoken that which
the histories of bygone ages have related."*
--Baha'u'llah
(Kitab-i-Aqdas: Proclamation of Baha'u'llah, p. 89)

"Behold! I make All things NEW!" (Rev. 21:5)

THE BEAST

1971 and 1996,

by Dr. Leland Jensen

An official Rendition by the Promised 7th Angel, who fulfills Biblical Prophecies, explained by 'Abdu'l-Baha as recorded in *Some Answered Questions*, also prophesied to come under different titles, such as "Blessed is He" who comes in 1963, explained by 'Abdu'l-Baha as recorded in *Baha'u'llah and the New Era*, the knight on the white horse, the Lamb, The Land, the return of Jesus the High Priest and by various names and titles as found in all Revelations of the Divine Manifestations.

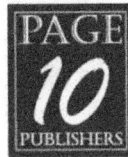

PAGE
10
PUBLISHERS

page10publishers.com
www.uhj.net
www.bupc.org

All Bible Quotes, King James Bible
Unless Otherwise Indicated

Cover Artwork
by M S

Introduction
by Harry Stroup (1971)

Drawing of Beast on page one
by Cloyce Little Light

Epilogue: Morrisites; Jesus in Prison (1999)
by Neal Chase

CONTENTS

CONTENTS

INTRODUCTION

The Baha'i Faith sets forth many seemingly incredible claims, but upon sincere and open minded investigation by the pure hearted seeker of truth, the veils of self are lifted from the eyes and the doors of the Kingdom of God are swung open. Of course the decision is then left up to the individual whether he or she wants to enter or not. This article written by Dr. Leland Jensen is just such a claim and should be considered as his Proclamation to the peoples. If investigated with an open mind one is assuredly captivated by the overwhelming insight into such an extensive field of material.

Now, as we all know, many people are claiming to be prophets, seers, and what have you; but are they really representing God, and if so, how can we be absolutely sure of this? There is very definitely a sure way of discerning whether or not these people are phonies or are actually who they claim to be. In the Holy Books, such as the Bible, the prophets of old prophesied of individuals who would make their appearance at given dates and described the events which would accompany these appearances. But, they did even more than this so that the peoples of today would not miss the ones who were Promised to come. They gave four distinct and undeniable facts as proof for the authenticity of these Promised individuals. These four proofs are, name, date, address, and profession, which are of great importance; for instance, if a man should hand you his business card, you would find on it these four facts and would be able to locate him from no matter where you were in the world. The same applies to the ones who have been prophesied in the Holy Books.

This man, Dr. Leland Jensen, shows the same type of proofs for himself to be the Joshua for today, through the words of the prophets of old, as Jesus gave for being the Messiah of His day. The proofs for Jesus being the Messiah were given as:

Name: Immanuel in Hebrew, Jesus in Greek, or God With Us in English (Isaiah 7:14).

Date: His crucifixion was given by Daniel in chapter 9 as 70 weeks or 490 days which becomes 490 years (Numbers 14:34) from the order to restore and rebuild Jerusalem, which was given in Ezra, chapter 7, as 457 B.C. Christ being 33 years of age at his crucifixion (457 + 33 = 490).

Address: As Bethlehem (Micah 5:2)

Profession: As the Savior, or to atone for iniquity   (Daniel 9:24-25).

AUTHENTICITY IS THE CRITERIA FOR BELIEVABILITY.

-- Harry Stroup

Gathering Unto the Throne

"Then he showed me the river of the water of life, bright as crystal, flowing from the throne of God and of the Lamb"

Revelation 22:1; 14:1,5

Baha'i International Gathering
Kamal, Perfection, 8-10, 160 BE
August 8-10, 2003 CE

Baha'is Under the Provisions of the Covenant

The Beast Is About To Be Dead

What Beast? The Beast that now rules the world! As you can see it has the body of a Leopard, feet of a Bear, mouth of a Lion and has Eagle's Wings. These are the symbols of today's Four World Powers. The Eagle is the symbol of the United States. See a dollar bill, or the Great Seal of the United States. The symbol of England is the Lion. The Bear is the symbol of Russia, and the Leopard, France. The Leopard became the symbol of France when Charlemagne conquered the Saxons. At that time the symbols of these Germanic tribes merged and became one, the symbol of France being the Panther, or Pard in French, was combined with the symbol of the Saxons which was a Lion, or Leo in Greek, making a Leopard the symbol of France.[1] This is the body of the Holy Roman Empire. These Four Beasts were prophesied and depicted in the seventh chapter of Daniel as a Lion with Eagle's wings, with the Eagle's wings being separated

---

[1]   "leopard, n. [< OF < LL < leopardus , leon lion + pardos panther]. pard, n. Archaic A leopard or panther. Old French parde", *The Reader's Digest Great Encyclopedic Dictionary*, pp. 775 and 979.

from the Lion and standing on its feet like a man. At one time the United States was a colony of England, but with the Declaration of Independence and the Revolutionary War that followed, the United States became separated from England. Daniel's next Beast is that of a Bear, which of course is Russia, and the Leopard is France (Daniel 7:4-6). THESE ARE THE FOUR SUPER POWERS — The Big Four.

ST. JOHN IN REVELATION SEES THESE BEASTS UNITED AS ONE BEAST

It has seven heads and ten horns, that has a body of a Leopard, feet of a Bear and a mouth of a Lion (Rev. 13:1-2). These four Atomic Powers became united into a single Beast under the United Nations Charter when they formed the United Nations. Unitedly they rule the world, in conjunction with the U.N. General Assembly, which gives the Beast its direction (Rev. 13:7). This General Assembly is composed of nations whose peoples are followers of the world's seven alive, revealed, apostate religions: 1. Hindu, 2. Buddhist, 3. Jewish, 4. Christian, 5. Muslim, 6. Zoroastrian, 7. Baha'i. The Head that had a "mortal wound, but its mortal wound was healed" (Rev. 13:3) is the Zoroastrian. At one time the Zoroastrian Civilization was the World Power. The Zoroastrian kings, Cyrus, Darius, Xerxes, and Artaxerxes ruled the world from the river in India to Greece which was then the Western World. During the Muslim invasion of Persia in the seventh century, almost all of this religious system was destroyed, but it still exists. There are but about one hundred thousand followers in the world today.

These Heads are "blasphemous" because these revealed religions became apostate, that is, they fell into the hands of man and he so changed these religions that they mean something quite different from that which was Revealed by God, and sent down to man through the mouth of His Holy Prophets — Manifestations. In the 17th chapter, verse 10 of Revelation, John refers to these Heads as being "seven kings, five of whom have fallen, one is, the other has not yet come, and when he comes he must remain only a little while". These kings are the dynasties, or the ones that took over and corrupted these seven religions. The "five whom have fallen" are the ones that took over and corrupted the Hindu, Buddhist, Jewish, Zoroastrian, and Islamic religions, for these dynasties are no longer in existence. For instance the dynasty that took over and corrupted Islam, was the Bani-Umayyad, and of course it does not exist today. The dynasty that took over and corrupted the Christian Faith however, is the "one is" for it is the one that "is". It started in the day of the Apostles and still exists today. This is the one that claims the chair of St. Peter (2 Thess. 2:1) and will continue to exist until it is destroyed by fire (Rev. 19:20-21). The only Christian religion in the world today that claims its dynasty goes all the way back to the Apostles and claims the chair of St. Peter is the Roman Catholic religion with its papacy, the false prophet in Revelation 19:20. Therefore, it is the "one that is".

The Head that appears last and is to remain but for a little while is the sans Guardian (without Guardian) Baha'i Faith, which became the seventh, ugly, blasphemous Head of this Beast in 1957 with the passing of the first Guardian, Shoghi Effendi, when the mass or majority of the Baha'is throughout the world chose to put the Covenant of Baha'u'llah — *Will and Testament of 'Abdu'l-Baha* — aside and became the followers of the former "Hands" of the Faith in their usurpation of the administration and institutions of the Faith and their fallacious direction, sans authority and Guardianship. In order to expedite their violation of the

Covenant — to eliminate the Guardianship of the Faith — they laid aside Shoghi Effendi's plan for the International Baha'i Council, with 'Abdu'l-Baha's son, Mason Remey, at its Head, to become a Baha'i World Court on Mt. Carmel, Haifa, Israel by 1963, with its body being elected later. They did this in spite of the wording of the *Will and Testament* (W&T) that they are not to deviate even a hairs breadth to the right or the left of the Covenant; or "Whoso obeyeth him not, ...hath not obeyed God" (W&T, p. 11). These "Hands" were appointed by Shoghi Effendi, who was appointed the first Guardian of the Faith in the *Will and Testament*, "All must be under his shadow and obey his command" (W&T, page 13). The only authority that they had was to protect the Cause of God from anyone beginning to oppose and protest against the Guardian, (see *Will and Testament*, p. 12 ff). They not only didn't protect the Faith from the violation of the Guardianship, but they were the prime movers in the violation. Thus, with this violation the Beast became complete with the appearance of its seventh ugly Head. With the setting up of a headless Universal House of Justice — injustice — under the direction of the violating "Hands" on Mt. Carmel, in 1963, in the stead of Shoghi Effendi's World Court with Mason Remey at its Head, these violating "Hands" had changed the last religion of God to mean something quite different from what He had sent down and the seventh ugly head of the Beast was complete (Isaiah 24:5).[2]

IT IS CALLED A BEAST BECAUSE IT IS NOT SPIRITUAL

Because of its perversity this Beast is not under the direction of God, therefore, it goes into perdition — utter destruction (Rev. 17:8, 11 and 19:20). It does not have the guidance of the "Glory of God" — Baha'u'llah — through the Universal House of Justice (UHJ) with both a legislative branch and an executive branch. Infallibility was conferred on the UHJ, which is these two branches together. The throne of God (Rev. 4:2) is the Davidic lineage, the throne of David which Baha'u'llah sat upon. The one who is seated upon the throne is the Davidic King (Baha'u'llah or His descendant), who is the Guardian of the Baha'i Faith and the executive branch of the UHJ, the Presidency — Head — of the Universal House of Justice (*Will and Testament of 'Abdu'l-Baha*, pp. 14-15). That is, for as long as there is life upon this planet, which may be for millions of years yet, there will be a Universal House of Justice with a living Guardian seated upon the throne of David at its Head. Baha'u'llah brought the Kingdom of God on earth as it is in Heaven (the Lord's Prayer, Matt. 6:9). Shoghi Effendi set up the first International Baha'i Council on Jan. 9, 1951. This was the UHJ in embryo. The "Hands" seized authority of the Faith in 1957 after Shoghi's death and this embryo was not born into the world. The second International Baha'i Council was born into the world exactly 40 years after Shoghi set up the first IBC, on Jan. 9, 1991. This second IBC will evolve through four stages; an International Baha'i Council, World Court, Supreme Tribunal and the Universal House of Justice.

The Beast with its blasphemous Heads must be destroyed. Because of its own perversity and lack of divine guidance it destroys itself. The United States itself has enough atomic destructive force to equal three thousand pounds of dynamite for every man, woman, and child

---

2   "The earth is also is defiled under the inhabitants therof; because they have transgressed the laws, changed the ordinance, **broken the everlasting covenant.**" — Isaiah

upon this planet. Plus it has the vehicles — missile — to carry this destruction to every part of the world (Zech. 5:1-5). The Bear, equals this destructive force and even surpasses it. The Lion has a cobalt bomb, which if exploded would destroy all life upon this earth.

HOW IT IS ABOUT TO DIE

There are to be four great waves of destruction. These are the four winds of destruction seen by John in his vision in the 7th chapter of Revelation. The first of these waves is the atomic war that is upon us. This was seen by him as "flashes of lightning, loud noises, peals of thunder, an earthquake, and heavy hail" (Rev. 11:19, 4:3, 8:5, & 16:18). The lightning is the atomic clash preceding the mushroom cloud. And the loud noise is the sound of the explosion, and the great hail is the fallout. Also see 2 Peter 3:10, Rev. 17:18, Rev. 16, Rev. 18:8, Rev. 19, Isaiah 24:6, and 2 Peter 3:7, 12).

One of the great waves will be from the wormwood or fallout.[3] Following the atomic war this fallout, not only itself will cause disease and suffering, but will render the food inedible. Two thirds of the people will be killed (Zech. 13:8). Their dead bodies will lie in the streets, and will not be able to be buried, because of the fallout contamination. Thus these decaying bodies will bring about new diseases that we don't even know about today.

The third of these waves of destruction will be an asteroid hitting the earth which will cause great tidal waves.

There will be a world wide revolution. The minorities that have long suffered at the hands of the establishment will arise and make quick work of their oppressors. All in all it will be the worst catastrophe that the world has ever had or ever will have (Matthew 24:21-22 and Isaiah 24:6).

The fourth wave of the catastrophe will be even worse than the other three put together: the earth's shifting crust (Rev. 18:21, Isaiah 13:13 and Isaiah 24:19). If it wasn't for the elect, there would be no flesh left alive on earth (Matthew 24:22). There will be crumpling up of mountain ranges, new continents will appear; there will be great inundations, and the whole geography of the earth will undergo a drastic change. The earth as we know it will come to an end.

THE EARTH'S SHIFTING CRUST

The crust of the earth is anywhere from 3 to 30 miles thick and is mostly solid rock, and encases the entire globe. Underneath this crust there is a layer of molten lava — magma — that is soft and slippery, which allows the crust to easily slide over the body. The mechanism that forces the crust to slide in a specific direction is the lopsided deposition of ice on the land in a polar region. Albert Einstein stated: "In a polar region there is a continual deposition of ice, which is not symmetrically distributed about the pole. The earth's rotation acts on these

---

3   Revelation 8:10-11. Chernobyl is the Russian-Ukranian word for "wormwood". See "The Bible adds a new dimension to Chernobyl accident," Serge Schmemaan, New York Times, Sun, August 3, 1986.

unsymmetrically deposited masses, and produces centrifugal momentum that is transmitted to the rigid crust of the earth. The constantly increasing centrifugal momentum produced in this way will, when it has reached a certain point, produce a movement of the earth's crust over the body and will displace the polar region toward the equator." (Forward to Charles Hapgood's *Earth's Shifting Crust*).

The continent of Antarctica is about twice the size of the United States, and has high mountain ranges like the Rocky Mountains. In the last 11,000 years, since the last crustal shift, there has been deposited on this continent a one half mile to one mile high layer of ice. This ice is unsymmetrically located and exerts a centrifugal pressure on the crust due to the force of the earth's rotation on its axis. This is now shoving the crust northward on the 115 degrees longitudinal meridian-Eastern Hemisphere. The Greenland ice cap although smaller is working in tandem with this and is shoving the crust in the Western Hemisphere southward. The more this movement continues the hotter becomes the magma (due to friction) and the more slippery it becomes; also the more eccentric becomes the Antarctic ice cap. The further that the center of Antarctica gets from the South Pole the greater becomes the centrifugal force. In addition to this there is deposited on this continent from fifty to one hundred feet of new ice each year. This ice cap is now bigger than the one — North American Ice Cap — that caused the crustal shift 11,000 years ago, that moved the North Pole from the Hudson Bay area to the Arctic Ocean, causing the receding of the Wisconsin Ice Age. The mammoths that were grazing on the plains of northern Siberia were quickly moved into the Arctic Circle, and were quickly frozen, thus preserving their flesh to this day. Antarctica was moved into the south polar region. Coal has been discovered 200 miles from the South Pole. In order for that continent to have coal deposits, it would have been necessary for it to have had a coniferous forest, like that which is now found in Montana.

At a specific preordained date, there will be a rapid slipping of the crust. The North Pole will move into the Lake Baikal area of Siberia. The United States will move southward about 2,000 to 3,000 miles toward the equatorial bulge and under a mile high of water. Just about everything in this country below 2,500 feet will be inundated. Thus, this is a terrifying picture of the birth of God's Kingdom on Earth as it is in Heaven.

THIS STONE WITH SEVEN EYES, A SHRINE

Deer Lodge, Montana, where this prison is located, this "Stone with Seven Eyes," will become a shrine, and a place of pilgrimage. The Kingdom of God will be firmly established here on earth. People will come from all over the world to pray at the site, where the Promised Joshua (Jesus) for our age was inhumanely, cruelly and illegally incarcerated. Everybody in that day will be believers.

A man standing with his family, perhaps with his little daughter holding on to his arm, may say, "Behold the stone wall with seven watch towers of the ancient prison of Montana." His daughter may say, "Daddy what is a prison?" He will reply, "That was an institution of the archaic past." All other disgraceful institutions of the kingdom of man will have also disappeared. War, hatred, prejudice, pillage, carnage, injustice, iniquities, tyranny and oppression will have ceased. Every man will sit under his own vine and fig tree (Zech. 3:10) and none will make him afraid. This world will have become another world, a paradise, a rose garden.

666, WHO IS HE?

The dragon in Revelation Twelve is the fourth beast of Daniel 7:7, (actually the fifth beast as the first separated into two beasts — the Lion and the Eagle). As prophesied, the dragon came to an end before the Beast with seven heads and ten horns of Revelation (Daniel 7:12). John said that the dragon gave over to the Beast his power, throne and great authority (Rev. 13:2). This took place with the collapse of the Caliphate and Sultanate of Islam. The dragon is described and prophesied in Revelation Twelve as looking somewhat like the Beast, having seven heads and ten horns and is also very ugly. The dragon started with the Bani-Umayyad, which was the dynasty that took over and corrupted Islam. The seven heads were the seven countries that the Bani-Umayyad had power over. These were Persia, Turkestan and Transoxania, the Middle East, Arabia, Egypt, North Africa, and Spain. The ten horns were: Abu Sufian and nine of his descendants, that were Umayyad Caliphs that ruled over these seven countries, Abu Sufian is "that beast" of Revelation 11:7, that at first vigorously opposed Islam and then gained control of it with his son Mu'awia becoming Caliph in 661 A.D. The number of this beast is 666 (Rev. 13:18). In reality it is 616, as explained in foot note (g) to Revelation 13:18 in the Revised Standard Version of the Bible: (g) = Other ancient authorities read "six hundred and sixteen". In 616 A.D. Abu Sufian became the Emir of Mecca — Chief of the Korish Tribe and of the Clan of Umayyad — and was Muhammad's and Islam's chief persecutor, causing Muhammad to flee Mecca. Muhammad went to Medina where he became the Head of State. Abu Sufian pursued him and made war on him (Rev. 11:7). There were a number of pitched battles with Muhammad coming off the victor. Finally Muhammad in 628 A.D. gained the victory over Mecca and Abu Sufian was obliged to become Muslim in 630 A.D. From that time onward, however, he plotted to take over Islam. Mu'awia, Abu Sufian's son, caused the killing of Ali, Muhammad's chosen successor. He then set himself up as Caliph, in Ali's stead, in 661 A.D.

THE DEATH OF THE DRAGON

The dragon became dismembered during the First World War, with the Ottoman Empire breaking up into a number of states, which then became colonies or protectorates of either France or England, thus giving their power and authority over the Beast (Rev. 12:2). The Sultanate had usurped the power and authority of the Caliphate and it came to an end in 1921, 1260 years after Mu'awia gained control of Islam in 661 A.D., 661 + 1260 = 1921 (see 'Abdu'l-Baha's explanation on page 79 in *Some Answered Questions* (SAQ), Chapter XIII).[4]

---

4   From the death of Ali in January of 661 A.D., when Mu'awia gained control, there are exactly 1260 years to the fall of the Ottoman Empire when the Christian Allies of the West set up the Interallied Control in Constantinople in January of 1921 A.D. (see H.G. Wells, *Outline of History*, p. 931) — when the dragon (the Islamic) "government evaporated".

THE TEN HORNS OF THE BEAST

After the Second World War the Islamic states that had once been part of the dragon, but had become colonies or protectorates of the Beast, gained their independence, and then became members of the United Nations. These ten countries, thus became the ten horns of the Beast. They are: Syria, Jordan, Lebanon, Iraq, Egypt, Sudan, Libya, Tunisia, Algeria, and Arabia. They will join with Russia for one hour during the atomic war (Rev. 17:12, 13), for they hate the whore who is seated upon the beast (Rev. 17:16). Being Muslim, they have an aversion to visible idols, and those that join gods to God. These countries have just recently been subjugated to countries that follow the trinitarian religion (Christians).

THE MARK OF THE BEAST
A LAMB WITH TWO HORNS

The dynasty, as already explained, that took over and corrupted Islam was the dragon. Islam is the religion of God that was sent down to man through the mouth of His Holy Prophet, Muhammad. After the dragon got control of this religion, however, it became an animal — a lamb with two horns — that spoke as a dragon (Rev. 13:11). The two horns of this beast are the two divisions of Islam, the Shiah and Sunni sects, that have the sun and the moon respectively as their symbols (Rev. 12:1).

These divisions came about through the action of the dragon — the Umayyad's taking over of the Caliphate. The Sunnis are those that backed the Umayyad's in their take-over, and the Shiahs are those that were in opposition. The Shiahs were the backers of Ali and the Imams. Later they also became corrupted, especially after the Imamate came to an end. The dragon had so corrupted Islam that almost nothing remained but fasting, prayer and the name. Almost all the laws of the Koran were laid aside, including the rights of the non-Muslims in the Islamic Empire. Therefore, unless one had the mark of the beast in the forehead and the right hand, his rights of citizenship were arbitrarily abrogated (Rev. 13:16, 17). Muslims pray five times a day and at specific times when they pray, no matter where they are, they touch their foreheads to the ground. In doing this they place their hand over their mouth to keep from breathing the dust. Thus, they have a dust mark on their forehead and on the back of their hand — the mark of the beast of Revelations 13:16.[5]

THE IMAGE OF THE BEAST

The image of the Beast with seven heads and ten horns, that is about to die, is the crucifix and that horrid picture that the Christians hang on their walls, which they acclaim to be the image of Christ, their incarnate god (Exodus 20:4). The monks of the fifth century, in order to

---

5   "The mark of them is on their foreheads from the traces of prostration. Such is their likeness in the Torah and their likeness in the Gospel." — The Victory Surah, XLVIII, verse 29, trans. Mohammed M. Pickthall, *The Meaning of the Glorious Koran.*

introduce idol worship into Christianity had these pictures to bleed, move and even to talk, and many miracles were attributed to them, and caused those that "would not worship the image of the Beast to be slain" (Rev. 13:15). Over a million Jews, Muslims, non-Christians, as well as some Protestant sects that had abolished the Crucifix, in the Holy Roman Empire were put to death, and in the most cruel manner in the Inquisition. And in our day 6,000,000 Jews and non-Christians were put to death in the gas chambers and incinerators of Germany.

THE WHORE

John saw a whore riding on the Beast (Rev. 17:3). This is the bitch that brought the Beast into existence. God pretty well explained through the mouth of His prophet Ezekiel, in chapter sixteen, that when His religion becomes apostate, it is then a whore. He portrays His pure revealed religion as a bride adorned for her husband (Rev. 21:2). Each of the religions revealed by God in its inception was like a pure and beautiful woman, but when each religion in its turn fell to the dynasty that got control of her and corrupted her, she became a whore. The false trinity doctrine with its accompanying incarnate god lie was that terrible corruption that turned the beautiful woman, the religion of Jesus, into that awful whore. This corruption is the weed that Jesus said is to grow so close to the grain that to pull it out you would pull out the grain itself. In fact, this lie (2 Thess. 2:11) is growing so close to the truth that it has become so intertwined with it, so that if anyone would have pulled it out at any point down from the days of the Apostles until the present time, there would have been no Christianity left. The one who planted this weed Jesus said, is Satan (Matthew 13:24-30, 37-42).

THE MAN OF SIN
THE SON OF PERDITION

This satan that planted the weed is the man of sin that corrupted the beautiful woman and made a whore out of her (2 Thess. 2:3). He started in the days of the apostles and is now being revealed (2 Thess. 2:7-8). He is the false prophet that comes in the name of Christ — Vicar of Christ — and deceives many, and is thrown alive into the lake of fire along with the Beast (Rev. 19:20). That is, he is destroyed along with the Beast in the approaching thermonuclear war.

THE ANTICHRIST

This man of sin is an anti-Christ. Martin Luther said: "The pope is the anti-Christ for he is against Christ." He is anti-Christ because he is anti-Messiah — anti-Anointed, he is against the lineage of Jesus the Christ. Christ means "anointed male sperm descendant of David". He took the Messiah of the Jews and made a god out of him. Then he took this god and joined him to God, making him the second person of a trinity, saying that Jesus is God, and that when he was born of Mary he was God incarnate. By doing this he denies that Jesus was anointed with the Holy Spirit from God, that which makes Jesus the Messiah — the anointed one —

the Christ — the anointed male sperm descendant of David. The Hebrew word Messiah when translated into Greek is christos — Christ — and when translated into English is anointed male sperm descendant of David. By saying that Jesus is God, he therefore could not be anointed by God. Therefore this man of sin is anti-Anointed — anti-Messiah — ANTI-CHRIST.

Jesus is neither God, nor is he a third part of God. What could be more blasphemous than to say that God is a man. Man is a creature of God, and Jesus said that he was the son of man — a man; and the scriptures give the name of the man that he is the son of (Luke 3:23, John 1:45). He was the Messiah, because he was anointed with the Holy Spirit. He was a Manifestation of God, because through the Holy Spirit he reflected God — like a mirror that is anointed with the rays of the sun reflects the sun. He was one of God's Revelators, a messenger. The appellation of "the son of God" refers to the Word, his message. He was a mouthpiece of God. He was a Speaker of the Word — the Message (John 1:1,14). He was a Major Prophet of God. Moses said, "The Lord your God will raise up for you a prophet like me from among you, from your brethren" (Deut. 18:15). The Lord said to Moses, "I will raise up for them a prophet like you from among their brethren; and I will put My words in his mouth, and he shall speak to them all that I command him" (Deut. 18:18). The scriptures say that this prophecy is of Jesus (John 1:45, Acts 3:22, 7:37).

THE BIRTH OF THE BEAST

This devil that corrupted this precious woman, the religion of Jesus, and then after foisting this harlot on the people of Christendom, brought the Beast into existence.

In the first part of the eighth century, about one hundred years after the advent of Islam, the whole eastern half of the Roman Empire fell to the Muslims. This consisted of Turkey, Egypt, North Africa and Spain as well as the whole Middle East, which is now Syria, Iraq, Jordan, Israel, and Lebanon. These people rapidly became Muslim, and there were three main reasons for their rapid conversion. First, those in the Middle East still possessed the Bible in the original tongue of Jesus. In these originals, Jesus named his successor Muhammad by name. This name was then translated into Greek as the Paraclete, and was later translated into English as the Comforter (KJV) and in the Revised Standard Version as Counselor. Second, the Christians of Egypt and North Africa were not trinitarian in belief, but this doctrine as well as the incarnate god lie was being forced on them by the Catholic Church. Third, the incessant charge of idolater against the Christians by the Jews and the Mohammedans, who had derived from the law of Moses and the Koran, immortal hatred of graven images and idol worship. The situation was grave. The whole Roman Empire of the East was gone and the capital, Constantinople, was surrounded by the great Islamic Empire, and it was ready to fall. If something was not done about idol worship in the Christian religion nothing would be left. The Emperor, Leo III, called a synod of the bishops of the Church and senators together, and they decided that idol worship in the Christian Church should be abolished. The worship of images had crept into the church since the fifth century by insensible degrees; by the eighth century it had attained the full magnitude of its abuse. The Greeks awoke to the fact that under the mask of Christianity they had returned to the idol worship of their fathers. Leo the Third issued two edicts against idol worship. The second prohibited the existence of all idols — pictures as well as statues.

Through this edict all the churches in the Capital and the provinces were cleansed from idolatry. But at that time Gregory the Second, the Roman Pontiff, was the man of sin. He wrote a letter to Emperor Leo III condemning him for his attack on idol worship, and he defended the images. This epistle is still in existence. It was written in 731 A.D. and it was the founder of the papal monarchy. It was a letter of revolt (2 Thess. 2:3), of the Roman Pontiff and the province of Italy, to the Roman Empire and the rest of Christendom.

After the cleavage and the setting up of the Holy Roman Empire, the debates and decrees of many provincial synods introduced the summons of a general council of the Christian religion (this council was acclaimed the seventh). This was convened during the time of Constantine V. Three hundred and thirty-eight bishops of Europe after serious deliberation of six months, pronounced and subscribed a unanimous decree that all visible symbols of Christ were either blasphemous or heretical; that image worship was a corruption of Christianity and a renewal of Paganism; that all such monuments of idolatry should be broken or erased. The Roman Catholics, that had separated themselves, did not attend or participate in this council.

The Papacy not only vested itself in the purple of the Roman Emperor and declared itself the temporal ruler, as well as the spiritual head of Christianity, but called itself the Vicar of Christ (substitute Christ or God, 2 Thess. 2:4).

Luther in breaking with the Papacy declared: "For at last I know that the Pope is the anti-Christ and his throne is that of satan himself" (D'aubigne, b, 6 chap. 9). When the Pope put on the purple, the whore, the trinitarian religion became clothed with purple and scarlet (Rev. 17:4), as the color of the cardinals is scarlet. The cup of abominations that she holds in her hand are all the perversions of Christian religion. One of the most dastardly is that of the crucifix, for there is nothing more odious and abominable than the making of an idol of an incarnate god (Exodus 20:4).

Pope Gregory II started the Holy Roman Empire in 731 A.D. Then the Papacy crowned Pepin, the King of France. Then it crowned Charlemagne, a descendant of Pepin and King of France, the Emperor of the Holy Roman Empire. Thus the body — the Leopard — of the Beast, that now rules the world, was born. The sword of Charlemagne brought Western Europe under the influence of the Holy Roman Empire.

ROME - BABYLON THE GREAT THE MOTHER OF HARLOTS

Rome is the city that is surrounded with "seven hills" (Rev. 17:9). It is also the city where the martyrdom of the early Christians took place, "the martyrs of Jesus" (Rev. 17:6). It is the city where the Pope signed the decree for the Crusade War that lasted for over two hundred years. It is also the city where the Pope signed the decree for the Spanish Inquisition in which over a million Jews, Mohammedans and Protestants were killed. It is the location of the Vatican that has more wealth in gold, jewels, and pearls than any two countries of Europe (Rev. 17:4,5). Its harlotry however, is the incarnate god lie and its accompanying invention of the fallacious doctrine of the trinity. It is the mother of harlots, because the Protestant sects that are in protestation to Rome espouse the same whoredom, making them daughter harlots. It is first for the fire (Rev. 18:8), and then it is to be inundated (Rev. 18:21).

The Date for the Beast to be Dead

The Beast is first to be burned with fire, then it is to be cut up and mutilated, and then it is to die! It has been allotted the same length of time to live as that of the dragon, 1260 years. The dragon came into existence in 660 A.D. and died 1260 years later in 1920.[6] From its beginning in 731 A.D. the Beast is given power to "exercise authority for forty-two months" (Rev. 13:5). Using the time scale of the Holy text, which is one day is as a year (Num. 14:34) these forty-two months are twelve hundred and sixty (1260) years. Thus the Beast was given the same amount of time as the Dragon had, to rule the world. By adding 1260 years to the year 731 A.D., we see that the Beast comes to its end in the year 1991 A.D. (731 + 1260 = 1991). This is the year that on January 9, 1991, the second International Baha'i Council was born into the world, that will go through four stages to become the Universal House of Justice.[7] The death of the Beast comes with the setting up of "The Kingdom of God on Earth as it is in Heaven". Then the Beast ceases to exercise any further authority.

Then Comes Joshua

World War III is on! The bombs can drop any time now! The four winds of destruction are held back only until the 144,00 come under **the everlasting Covenant** (Rev. 7:1, 2, 3, 14:3, Isaiah 24:5, 6).

Each of the religions of God have had a Joshua. Moses took Hoshea and called him Joshua (Num. 13:16), which means Yahweh is salvation, or God saves. Moses was the root and Joshua the branch. In Islam, Muhammad was the root and Ali the branch — the law and teachings of Muhammad, and the explanations and commentaries of Ali (see 'Abdul-Baha, SAQ, Chapter XI). Ali was the same as that of Joshua, he promoted the teachings and laws that Muhammad established. In the Babi religion it was the Bab and Quddus. I am the Joshua for today, for the second and last gathering of the tribes of Israel.

When I, "the land" = Leland, on April 29, 1971, made my Proclamation, that I fulfilled the prophecies for the Promised Joshua (Jesus) for our day, I fulfilled the prophecy for the name of Joshua, "the land" = Le land (Zech. 3:9). I fulfilled the prophecy for the address of Joshua, for no matter which way I turn, I have this "stone with seven eyes" before me (Zech. 3:9), that is located in the mountains of the northwest (Isaiah 49:11, 12). I fulfilled the prophecy of the dirty garment, for I am incarcerated illegally on just that type of charge (Zech. 3:3, 4). I fulfilled the prophecies of the dates for the coming of the Promised one for today (Dan. 12:12). 'Abdu'l-

---

6   Taken from 660 A.D., when Mu'awia set himself up as Caliph in Damascus in opposition to Ali, while Ali was still alive, there are exactly 1260 years until August 10, 1920 to the Treaty of Sevres when the Ottoman Empire collapsed giving up all their authority and claim to the rule and power of the territories of the entire East. The death of the dragon is taken from both 660 A.D. and 661 A.D., giving 1260 years to 1920/1921 A.D. for the death of the dragon. Both dates are correct.

7   This also marks the same exact time for the start of the Gulf War with Iraq (January, 1991 A.D.) spoken of in the book of Revelation: "Loose the four angels [holding back the four winds of destruction] which are bound at the **Great River Euprates** [which flows through Iraq]. And the four angels were loosed, which were prepared for an hour, and a day, and a month, and a year, for to slay the third part of men [1/3rd of mankind]" (Rev. 9:14-15, 7:1-3).

Baha said that the 1335 is to be figured from the start of the Muslim era, which started with Muhammad's victory in 628 A.D. (1335 + 628 = 1963). On that date I fulfilled the prophecy of having satan accuse or resist me (Zech. 3:1), for I was elected to an Assembly, which was called by the Guardian, and to which a man by the name of Rex King was also elected. He so resisted me as to stifle me in my service to the Cause, and he so accused me as to have the other members of that Assembly turn against me. Later in an epistle, the Guardian of the Faith rebuked this man, and proclaimed him to be the satan of our era (Zech. 3:2).

I also fulfilled the prophetic dates enshrined in the King's Chamber of the Great Pyramid. The 100 Red Granite slabs lining the walls of the King's Chamber represent the 100 year period from Baha'u'llah's Declaration in 1863 to my having satan at my right hand to accuse me in 1963. When I fulfilled the prophecy of the 108 Red Granite slabs comprising the floor of the King's Chamber, which represents the 108 year period between Baha'u'llah's Declaration to my own, I started to fulfill the occupation of Joshua. I drew my sword against the wicked and profane Beast, the harlot, the man of sin, and the false prophets (Eph. 6:17, Rev. 19:15). I started to raise up God's Heavenly Army (Rev. 19:19) — the elect (Matthew 24:22) — the chosen (Rev. 17:14) — the 144,00 (Rev. 7:4, 14:1,3) — the Legions of the Covenant (*World Order of Baha'u'llah*, p 17) — and the Tribes of Jacob (Isaiah 49:6), for I am "His servant, that is to bring Jacob back to God, and that Israel might be gathered to Him" (Isaiah 49:5). I am the High Priest in the Sanctuary — King's Chamber (Zech. 3:1).

From where did I start calling forth this Heavenly Army — God's Chosen? From out of this prison, that is surrounded by the "stone with seven eyes"; "saying to the prisoners, come forth, to those who sit in darkness, appear" (Isaiah 49:9); "to bring the prisoners from the dungeon" (Isaiah 42:7), and those that have been hidden in prisons and have ignominiously been put in the "hole" (Isaiah 42:22). Where is the prison from whence the Elect comes? They come from afar, from the mountains of the Northwest, from "the land" of Syene (Isaiah 49:11, 12, 13), for I am Leland, I am "the land" of Syene, as explained in the next 3 subtitles.

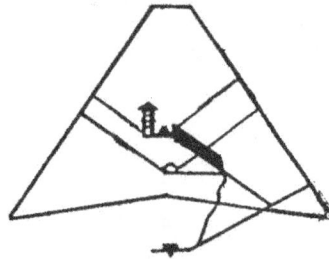

THE PROPHETIC PYRAMID
THE FOREMOST OF THE 7 WONDERS OF THE WORLD

The Great Pyramid of Gizeh first came to the attention of the scientific world when Sir Isaac Newton predicted that the length of the ancient cubit of Egypt and Israel could be found in this structure. Scientists soon found that almost all of the facts concerning the earth and its relation to the universe were also represented in this edifice; such as, the size of the earth, its circumference, its diameter, its weight, and its distance from the sun, etc., etc.. Thus, this monument soon found its way onto the dollar bill. In the place of the Cap Stone they put the all seeing eye, which represents its prophetic nature (Isaiah 19:19,20).

On the reverse of the Great Seal of the United States of America is the Great Pyramid. According to Manly P. Hall, an expert on Masonic Lore, not only were many of the founders of the U.S. government, Masons, but they received aid from a secret and august body existing in Europe, which helped them to establish the United States for a "peculiar and particular purpose known only to the initiate few". The Great Seal, says Hall, was the signature of this exalted body, and the unfinished pyramid on the reverse side "is a trestleboard setting forth symbolically the task to the accomplishment of which the U. S. government was dedicated from the day of its inception". It was related that the Eagle was apparently intended to represent a phoenix. As the legendary phoenix bird represented by ancient Egyptians as living for centuries, then being consumed in fire by its own act, and rising in youthful freshness from its own ashes; so the United States will be consumed in fire by the oncoming thermonuclear war. From its ashes will arise a Spiritual America. It will be the most chastened of all the nations. Where it is now a Beast, it will become a living creature (Rev. 4:7, RSV) and lead all nations spiritually. Its spiritual destiny is represented by the Pyramid on the back side of the Great Seal, and on the back side of the dollar bill. This spiritualization is represented by the prophetic aspect of the Great Pyramid and these prophetic aspects are enshrined in its inner passage ways and chambers.

Prophetic dates for the Advent of those sent by God are indicated by points in the passage-ways, with each Pyramid (P) inch representing one solar year. At the end of the Passage-way, at the Altar (or Great Step), from there on each P. inch represents one Baha'i month; and the Red Granite Blocks covering the floor and lining the walls of the Holy of Holies (King's Chamber) represents one solar year.

The 1485.5 P. inches from the start of the Ascending Passageway to the start of the Gallery of Religions (Grand Gallery) represents the 1485 years and 6 months from the Exodus of Moses, or Israel, on March 21, 1456 B.C. to the start of the ministry of Jesus at his Baptism on Sept. 22, 30 A.D. Descending down the Ascending passageway from the Gallery of Religions 29.718 inches you come to the Zero Point, the birth of Jesus, in 1 A.D./1 B.C. and the start of the Christian calendar. Ascending upward from the Zero Point 1843.218 P. inches you come to the end of the Gallery of Religions at the Alter, marking the end of the Christian Era and the start of the Baha'i Era and calendar, on March 21, 1844 A.D. The Baha'i Era and calendar was inaugurated by the Bab who made his Proclamation on May 23, 1844 A.D. This date exactly corresponds with the date given in the Bible (Daniel 8:13-14) for the return of Christ and the cleansing of the Sanctuary. It was exactly 2300 years from the Edict of King Artaxerxes, on March 21, 457 B.C., to restore and rebuild Jerusalem (Ezra 7:9) to

March 21, 1844 A.D. This has been acclaimed by many Biblical scholars, such as William Miller. The Sanctuary was cleansed by the blood of the Bab on the Altar just inside the Door of the Sanctuary; and by the blood of ten thousand of his followers in Glorious martyrdom, during the years represented by length of the Altar in the Pyramid.

The Bab, meaning Door or Gate, closed the door to the prophetic age and opened the door to fulfillment. His Revelation was of the potency of the Sanctuary and he is therefore the return of Jesus to earth in the Sanctuary, to which he had entered in heaven (Heb. 9:24). Like John the Baptist, he prepared the way for the Advent of the "Glory of the Lord" — Baha'u'llah (see the 43rd chapter of Ezekiel).

The new calendar instituted by the Bab, for the New Age, has 19 days to the month, and 19 months to the year, and 4 intercalary days, with leap years having five (one year = 19 months plus 4 1/4 intercalary days). Therefore there are 19.2232 Baha'i months in one solar year.[8]

Because each P. inch from the Altar on represents one Baha'i month of 19 days and there are 19.2232 Baha'i months in one solar year, the 366.8856407 P. inches from the start of the Altar to the Holy of Holies represents 19 years 31 days (366.8856407 divided by 19.2232 = 19.08547 or @ 19 1/12). It was 19 years 31 days from the vernal equinox (Naw Ruz) of March 21, 1844 to when Baha'u'llah entered the Garden of Ridvan on April 21, 1863 where He made His proclamation (see *God Passes By*, p. 148).

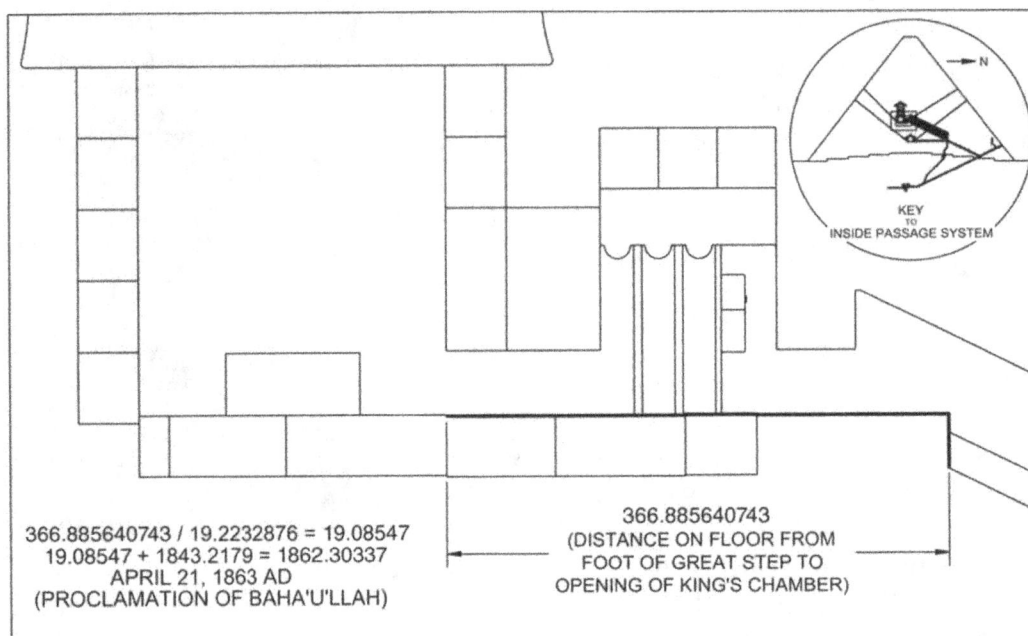

KEY
TO
INSIDE PASSAGE SYSTEM

366.885640743 / 19.2232876 = 19.08547
19.08547 + 1843.2179 = 1862.30337
APRIL 21, 1863 AD
(PROCLAMATION OF BAHA'U'LLAH)

366.885640743
(DISTANCE ON FLOOR FROM
FOOT OF GREAT STEP TO
OPENING OF KING'S CHAMBER)

---

8   For more on the Baha'i Calendar see *The Baha'i World Vol. XII, 1950-1954*, pp. 553-554.

DIAGRAM #1
PYRAMID OF GIZA

"THE BLUEPRINT OF GOD"
FOR THE MAKING OF "MAN IN OUR IMAGE" - MANIFESTATIONS OF GOD - (GENESIS 1:26) SEE ISAIAH 19:19. IT IS HIS CHRONOLOGICAL TIME-SCALE ERECTED 5400 YEARS AGO, FOR THE ADVENTS OF HIS MANIFESTATIONS AND OTHER HOLY ONES SENT BY HIM. IT IS THE PATHWAY OF GOD TAKING MAN FROM THE STONE-AGE (IN THE IMAGE OF ANIMAL) TO THE ESTABLISHMENT OF THE KINGDOM OF GOD "ON EARTH AS IT IS IN HEAVEN." THEN ALL MEN WILL BE IN THE IMAGE OF GOD, SEE REVELATION CHAPTERS 21 AND 22.

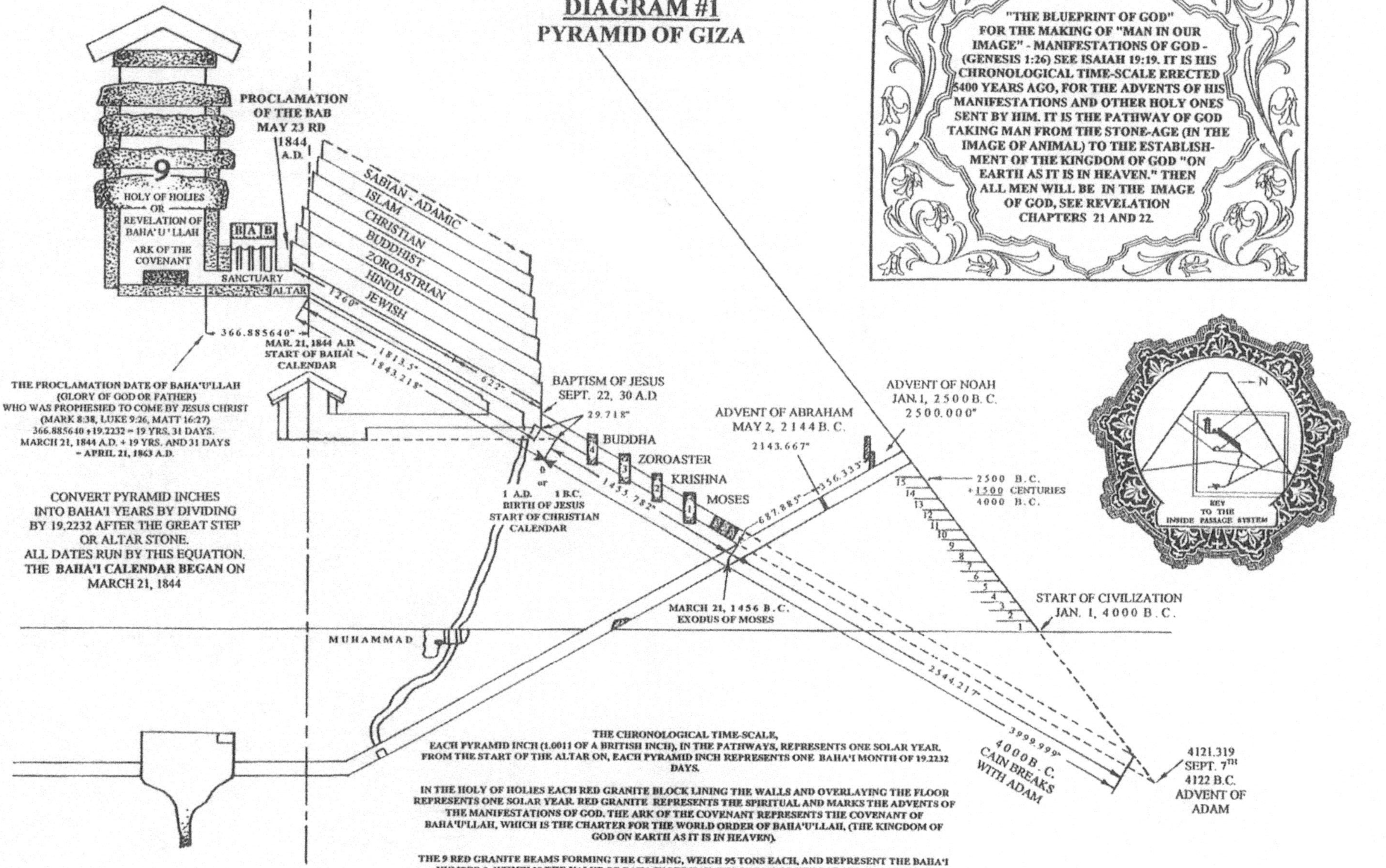

PROCLAMATION OF THE BAB MAY 23 RD 1844 A.D.
9
HOLY OF HOLIES OR REVELATION OF BAHA'U'LLAH
ARK OF THE COVENANT
B A B
SANCTUARY
ALTAR
SABIAN - ADAMIC
ISLAM
CHRISTIAN
BUDDHIST
ZOROASTRIAN
HINDU
JEWISH
1260"
366.885640"
MAR. 21, 1844 A.D. START OF BAHA'I CALENDAR
1813.5"
1843.218"
622"
THE PROCLAMATION DATE OF BAHA'U'LLAH (GLORY OF GOD OR FATHER) WHO WAS PROPHESIED TO COME BY JESUS CHRIST (MARK 8:38, LUKE 9:26, MATT 16:27) 366.885640 ÷ 19.2232 = 19 YRS. 31 DAYS. MARCH 21, 1844 A.D. + 19 YRS. AND 31 DAYS = APRIL 21, 1863 A.D.
BAPTISM OF JESUS SEPT. 22, 30 A.D.
29.718"
0 or 1 A.D. 1 B.C. BIRTH OF JESUS START OF CHRISTIAN CALENDAR
BUDDHA
ZOROASTER
KRISHNA
MOSES
4
3
2
1
1455.782"
CONVERT PYRAMID INCHES INTO BAHA'I YEARS BY DIVIDING BY 19.2232 AFTER THE GREAT STEP OR ALTAR STONE. ALL DATES RUN BY THIS EQUATION. THE BAHA'I CALENDAR BEGAN ON MARCH 21, 1844
ADVENT OF ABRAHAM MAY 2, 2144 B.C.
2143.667"
687.885"
356.333"
ADVENT OF NOAH JAN.1, 2500 B.C. 2500.000"
2500 B.C.
+1500 CENTURIES
4000 B.C.
15
14
13
12
11
10
9
8
7
6
5
4
3
2
1
START OF CIVILIZATION JAN. 1, 4000 B.C.
MARCH 21, 1456 B.C. EXODUS OF MOSES
MUHAMMAD
2544.217"
3999.999"
4000 B.C. CAIN BREAKS WITH ADAM
4121.319 SEPT. 7TH 4122 B.C. ADVENT OF ADAM
N
KEY TO THE INSIDE PASSAGE SYSTEM

THE CHRONOLOGICAL TIME-SCALE,
EACH PYRAMID INCH (1.0011 OF A BRITISH INCH), IN THE PATHWAYS, REPRESENTS ONE SOLAR YEAR. FROM THE START OF THE ALTAR ON, EACH PYRAMID INCH REPRESENTS ONE BAHA'I MONTH OF 19.2232 DAYS.

IN THE HOLY OF HOLIES EACH RED GRANITE BLOCK LINING THE WALLS AND OVERLAYING THE FLOOR REPRESENTS ONE SOLAR YEAR. RED GRANITE REPRESENTS THE SPIRITUAL AND MARKS THE ADVENTS OF THE MANIFESTATIONS OF GOD. THE ARK OF THE COVENANT REPRESENTS THE COVENANT OF BAHA'U'LLAH, WHICH IS THE CHARTER FOR THE WORLD ORDER OF BAHA'U'LLAH, (THE KINGDOM OF GOD ON EARTH AS IT IS IN HEAVEN).

THE 9 RED GRANITE BEAMS FORMING THE CEILING, WEIGH 95 TONS EACH, AND REPRESENT THE BAHA'I NUMBER 9, WHICH IS THE VALUE OF BAHA IN PERSIAN. THE VALUE OF THE BAB IS 5, THUS, THE 95 REPRESENTS BAHA'U'LLAH AND THE BAB.

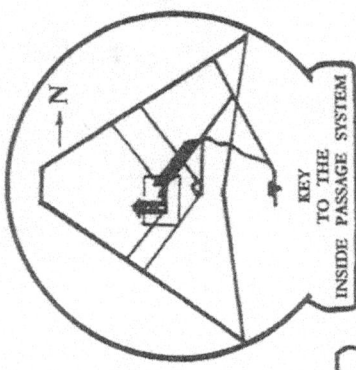

KEY TO THE INSIDE PASSAGE SYSTEM

DIAGRAM #2
KINGS CHAMBER, ANTECHAMBER, AND GRAND GALLERY OF LIGHT

CONVERT PYRAMID INCHES INTO BAHA'I YEARS BY DIVIDING BY 19.2232. AFTER THE GREAT STEP OR ALTAR STONE, ALL DATES RUN BY THIS EQUATION. THE BAHA'I CALENDAR BEGAN ON MARCH 21, 1844

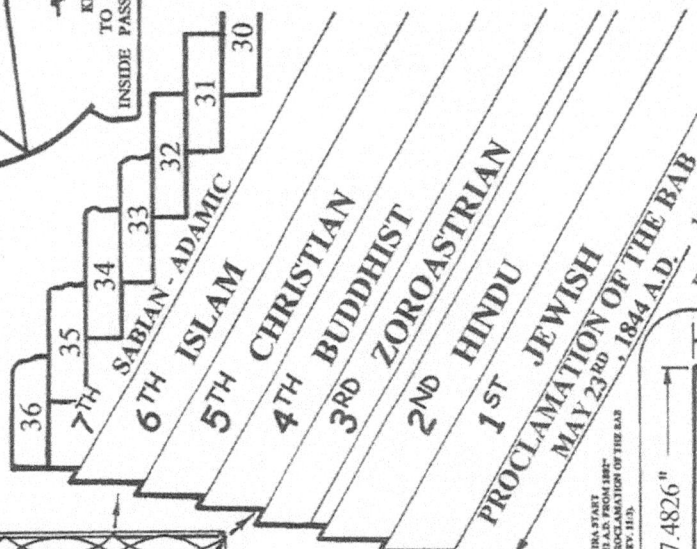

30
31
32
33
34
35
36

7TH SABIAN - ADAMIC
6TH ISLAM
5TH CHRISTIAN
4TH BUDDHIST
3RD ZOROASTRIAN
2ND HINDU
1ST JEWISH

PROCLAMATION OF THE BAB MAY 23RD, 1844 A.D.

THE DATES FOR THE ADVENTS OF THE MANIFEST-ATIONS OF THE 7 REVEALED RELIGIONS (ADAM, MOSES, KRISHNA, ZOROASTER, BUDDHA, CHRIST AND MUHAMMAD).

THEY PROPHESIED THE ADVENTS OF THE BAB AND BAHA'U'LLAH, AND APPEAR IN THE 7 OVERLAYS OF THE GRAND GALLERY OF LIGHT, FURTHER DETAIL IN DIAGRAM #1

THE BAB
THE DOOR
THE GATE (EZEKIEL 43:1 TO 7)

SANCTUARY

8TH BABI

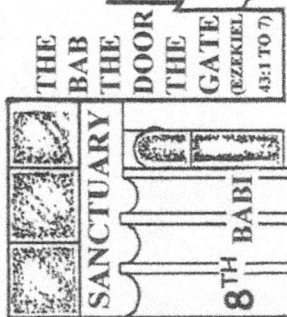

ALTAR

127.4826"

163.3979"

366.885640"

WHEN YOU SUBTRACT THE BEHRA START (OF THE MUSLIM CALENDAR) 622 A.D. FROM 1882" YOU HAVE THE DATE OF THE PROCLAMATION OF THE BAB 1260 A.H. OR MAY 23, 1844 A.D. (REV. 11:3).

35.915"

1882" OR 1260 A.H.

IT IS 1882" FROM THE BAPTISM OF JESUS TO THE GATE OR THE PROCLAMATION OF THE BAB.

1843.218" FROM JESUS TO PROCLAMATION OF THE BAB.

MARCH 21, 1844 A.D. OR 1260 A.H. START OF BAHA'I CALENDAR

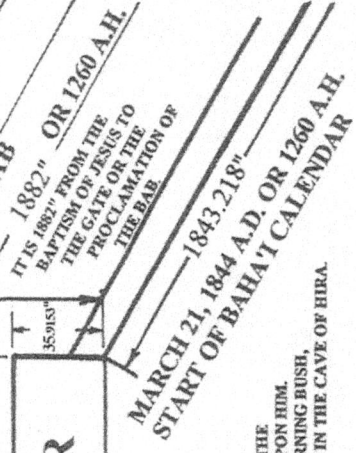

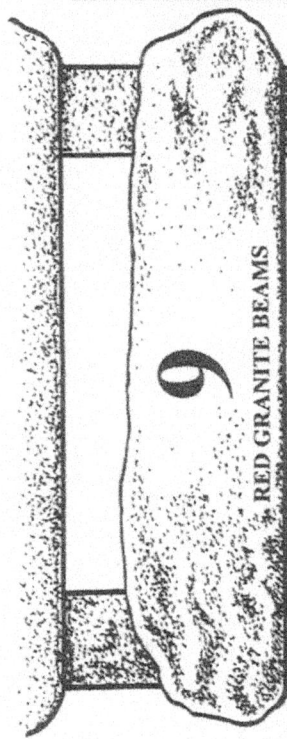

9
RED GRANITE BEAMS

HOLY OF HOLIES

100
RED
GRANITE
BLOCKS
BLOCKS

THE PROMISED HIGH PRIEST, JOSHUA, (3RD CHAPTER OF ZACHARIAH), ALONE STANDS IN THE HOLY OF HOLIES FOR HE ALONE IS PROPHESIED TO COME BY THE RED GRANITE BLOCKS AND BEAMS LINING THE HOLY OF HOLIES.

THE 100 BLOCKS LINING THE WALLS PLUS THE DATE OF THE PROCLAMATION OF BAHA'U'LLAH GIVES THE DATE THAT SATAN STARTED TO OPPOSE HIM (100 + APRIL 21, 1863 A.D.). THE 108 BLOCKS OVERLAYING THE FLOOR, PLUS THE DATE OF THE PROCLAMATION OF BAHA'U'LLAH, PLUS THE 9 DAYS REPRESENTED BY THE 9 BEAMS FORMING THE CEILING PROPHETICALLY GIVES THE DATE THAT THE PROMISED JOSHUA MADE HIS PROCLAMATION (108 + APRIL 21, 1863 A.D. + 9 DAYS = APRIL 29, 1971 A.D.).

THE HIGH PRIEST IN THE HOLY OF HOLIES IS THE SOLE CONTACT BETWEEN ISRAEL (BAHA'I) AND GOD. HE ESTABLISHES THE THIRD PART OF THE COVENANT OF MOSES (DEUT. 30TH CHAPTER) IN THE HOLY OF HOLIES, WHICH IS THE COVENANT OF BAHA'U'LLAH. FOR HE BRINGS FORTH THE BRANCH - GUARDIAN - THE MAIN PROVISION OF THE COVENANT. THUS, JOSHUA IS THE PROMISED GATHERER PROPHESIED TO COME IN CHAPTER 49 OF ISAIAH, AND 7 AND 14 OF REVELATION.

9TH BAHA'I

COVENANT OF BAHA'U'LLAH

108 RED GRANITE BLOCKS

APRIL 21st, 1863 A.D.

THE PROCLAMATION DATE OF BAHA'U'LLAH (GLORY OF GOD OR FATHER) WHO WAS PROPHESIED TO COME BY JESUS CHRIST (MARK 8:38, LUKE 9:26, MATT 16:27)

366.885640 ÷ 19.2232 = 19 YRS. 31 DAYS.

MARCH 21, 1844 A.D. + 19 YRS. AND 31 DAYS = APRIL 21, 1863 A.D.

163.3979" ÷ 19.2232 = 8.5 YEARS OR HALFWAY THRU YEAR 9 OF THE BAHA'I ERA. 8.5 YEARS + 1843.218 YEARS = 1851.718 YEARS, OR SEPT. 21, 1852 A.D,

THE DATE THAT BAHA'U'LLAH WAS PLACED IN THE DUNGEON AND THE HOLY SPIRIT DESCENDED UPON HIM. IT WAS SIMILAR TO THAT OF MOSES AT THE BURNING BUSH, JESUS AT THE RIVER JORDAN, AND MUHAMMAD IN THE CAVE OF HIRA.

THE GARDEN OF ROSES

During a twelve day period, which is designated the Ridvan period, in the Garden of Ridvan (Roses) just outside of the city of Baghdad, Baha'u'llah, literally meaning "Glory of God", when translated into English, made His Declaration, that He was the Promised "Son of Man" in the "Glory of God" that the world was waiting for, as prophesied to come in the Bible and other revealed religions (Mark 8:38, Rev. 21:11, 23, Ezek. 43:1-7, Isaiah 35:1, 2). His Revelation was that of the son of Man in the potency of the Father, and is therefore, the return of Christ in the Holy of Holies. His Revelation — laws, ordinances and teachings — are to establish the Christ Promised Kingdom of God on earth as it is in heaven.

Baha'u'llah entered the Garden of Ridvan on the afternoon of April 21, 1863 and left the Garden on May 2, 1863. Both the first day and the last day are designated as Baha'i Holy Days. The ninth day of Ridvan is also designated a Baha'i Holy Day and for no previously known reason. Besides being the numerical value of Baha, 9 represents completion and is the Baha'i number, and is the 9th revealed religion.[9] This 9 is represented in the Holy of Holies by the 9 massive Red Granite Beams comprising the ceiling of the Holy of Holies in the Great Pyramid. From the ninth day of Ridvan of Baha'u'llah's Proclamation in the Garden of Ridvan to my Proclamation to Harry Stroup with this "stone of seven eyes" before me, that I was the Promised Joshua of the third chapter of Zechariah, on the ninth day of Ridvan, April 29, 1971 was just exactly 108 years. These 108 years are represented in the Holy of Holies by the 108 red Granite Rock slabs that came from Syene and comprise the floor. From the Ridvan Period in 1863 to the Ridvan period in 1963 at which time I was a delegate and attended a convention called by the Guardian, and was elected to an Assembly of which satan was also elected, and was at my right hand to oppose and resist me was exactly 100 years. These 100 years are represented in the King's Chamber by the 100 Red Granite Rock Slabs that lines the walls of this chamber.

THE RETURN OF JESUS STANDING IN THE HOLY OF HOLIES

After entering the Holy of Holies the prophetic prophecies for the Advent of Joshua (Jesus), the High Priest, standing in the Holy of Holies before the Ark of the Covenant, is represented in the Great Pyramid by the red granite Rock Slabs lining the walls and comprising the floor, and by the massive Red Granite Rock Beams comprising the ceiling. The Pyramid is constructed with limestone blocks, which were water formed, and were quarried near the site. The Holy of Holies however, which represents the Revelation for the Kingdom of God on earth, is lined with Red Granite, which is fire-born and represents the Spiritual. These highly polished rock slabs that are so perfectly cut and honed, that they fit so close together that a razor blade cannot be inserted between them, prophesy the date of the coming of Joshua (Jesus), for Isaiah

---

9   Baha = 2 + 1 + 5 + 1 = 9. B=2, A=1, H=5, in Persian/Arabic Abjad reckoning, similar to Hebrew/Greek, Gematria, where all letters also represent numbers.

tells us the regathered Israel would come from the mountains of the northwest and from "the land" of Syene (Isaiah 49:12). They were quarried, cut, honed, and polished at the quarry at Syene. They were then placed on barges and floated down the River Nile to its Delta, the site of the Pyramid, which today is several miles southwest of Cairo. They then were taken and placed in against the walls and laid over the floor of the Holy of Holies, of this Great Temple of Light. As these Red Granite Blocks prophesy the High Priest in the Holy of Holies and they come from Syene, therefore, "the land" — Leland — who is the Promised Joshua (Jesus) of Zechariah prophecy is also "the land" of Syene for these blocks that come from Syene accurately prophesy the date of his Advent.

Joshua, Jeshua, and Jehoshua are Hebrew for the Greek Iesous or Jesus. They all have the same meaning. As the prophecies for the Advent of Joshua (Jesus) in the third chapter of Zechariah, and the prophecies for the Advent of the High Priest represented by the Red Granite Blocks in the Holy of Holies were not fulfilled by Jesus of Nazareth, they then refer to his second coming, for he also was a High Priest, not after the order of Aaron, but "being designated by God a High Priest after the order of Melchizedek"(Hebrews 5:10). He is now standing in the Holy of Holies regathering Israel, the elect, the chosen of God, the 144,000.[10]

THE RESTORED TEMPLE

The Advents of the Bab and Baha'u'llah are prophesied by name and address by Ezekiel in his prophecies for the Advent of the restored Temple: "Afterward he brought me to the Bab (gate), the Bab facing east. And behold, Baha'u'llah (the Glory of God) of Israel came from the east; and the sound of his coming was like the sound of many waters; and the earth shone with his Baha'i (Glory). And the vision I saw was like the vision which I had seen when he came to destroy the city, and like the vision which I had seen by the river Chebar; and I fell upon my face. As Baha'u'llah (the Glory of God) entered the temple by the Bab (Gate) facing east, the Spirit lifted me up, and brought me into the inner court; and behold, Baha'u'llah (the Glory of God) filled the temple. While the man was standing beside me, I heard one speaking to me out of the temple; and he said to me, 'Son of man, this is the place of my throne and the place of the soles of my feet, where I will dwell in the midst of the people of Israel for ever. And the house of Israel shall no more defile my holy name...'" (Ezek. 43:1-7). Ezekiel didn't speak English but wrote his prophecies in Aramaic; therefore he didn't use the English word gate as found in your Bible. He was in captivity in Babylon at the time, of which is now part of Persia. The word for gate in his language was "Bab", and for Glory of God, "Baha'u'llah".

The Bab made his proclamation in that part of Persia that was Babylon in the time of Ezekiel and this is "facing east". Baha'u'llah as a religious prisoner of the Turkish and Persian

---

10   "And they [144,000] sung a New Song [explanations of the Lamb] before **the throne,** and before the four beasts, and the elders: and no man could learn that song but the hundred and forty and four thousand, which were redeemed from the earth...These [144,000] were redeemed from among men, being firstfruits unto God and to the Lamb. And in their mouth was found no guile: for they are without fault before **the throne of God**" (Rev. 14:3-5).

Empires "came from the east" (Tehran) to Mt. Carmel, Israel (Isaiah 35:2). His message was like "the sound of many waters", as waters applies to all people. His revelation is for the establishing the oneness of mankind. When Ezekiel saw the Bab and Baha'u'llah, in his vision, he fell upon his face in adoration to these two Manifestations of God. With the spread of the Baha'i Faith throughout the world "the earth shone with His Baha'i (Glory)". This Temple — the Bab and Baha'u'llah — is the place of the throne of God for it is through the Revelation of Baha'u'llah that God will rule this earth, thus, the Kingdom of God on earth as it is in heaven as prayed for in the Lord's prayer.

Jesus who also spoke Aramaic also prophesied the Advent of Baha'u'llah by name: "For whoever is ashamed of me and of my words in this adulterous and sinful generation, of him will the Son of man also be ashamed, when he comes in Baha'u'llah with the holy angels" (Mark 8:38).

When the disciples asked Jesus the Christ when he was going to come again (Matthew 24:3), he told them to turn to Daniel where he speaks of the abomination of desolation standing in the Holy place (sanctuary) and they would have the date for his return (Matthew 24:15). At the time of Daniel, Jerusalem was desolate because of the Jews abominable practice of Idolatry. With the edict of Artaxerxes recorded in the seventh chapter of Ezra in 457 B.C. Jerusalem was rebuilt and its desolation came to an end. From that order it was 2300 years to March 21, 1844 the Advent of the Bab: the return of Jesus in the Sanctuary.

In the 12th chapter Daniel also speaks of the abomination of desolation, and here he gives three dates for the return of Jesus. The first is recorded in the 7th verse as 3 1/2 times. A time is a cycle or circle, which has 360 degrees. 3 1/2 x 360 = 1260. This 1260 is also recorded in the 11th and 12th chapters of Revelation for the return of Jesus. The Bab (the return of Jesus in the Sanctuary) made his Proclamation on May 23rd, 1844 in Shiraz, Persia where the Muslim calendar is used in place of the Christian and May 23rd 1844 was 1260 A.H.. The next date given by Daniel for the return of Christ is recorded in the 11th verse as 1290. It was just exactly 1290 years from the Proclamation of Muhammad to the Proclamation of Baha'u'llah, the return of Christ in the Glory of the Father (Mark 8:38), giving a Revelation of the potency of the Father (the Holy of Holies; the presence of God on earth). Christ is not the last name of Jesus but means anointed male sperm descendant of David in English. As Jesus was anointed by the Holy Spirit and a descendant of David making Him the Christ in the potency of the Son of God (Matthew 3:16), so the Holy Spirit descended upon Baha'u'llah making Him the Christ bringing a revelation in the potency of the Glory of God, or Father — Baha'u'llah. The third date given by Daniel, for "Blessed is he who waits and comes to the 1335 days" that is recorded in the 12th verse refers to the next coming of Jesus, the High Priest, standing in the Holy of Holies. It was just exactly 1335 years from the victory of Muhammad in 628 A.D. to the Advent of Joshua (Jesus), the High Priest in Ridvan 1963 A.D., standing in the Holy of Holies.

These prophecies in the Bible for the Advent of the restored Temple — the return of Jesus Christ — is illustrated in the road map recorded by God in the Pyramid "in the midst of Egypt", which was built at the borders of upper and lower Egypt (Isaiah 19:19). It is "a sign and witness" to the prophecies recorded in the Bible (Isaiah 19:20). The upper passageways bring us to the restored Temple; the Altar, the Bab, the Sanctuary, the Holy of Holies (the presence of the Glory of God-Baha'u'llah), the Ark of His Covenant, and the High Priest Joshua (Jesus) standing before the Ark of the Covenant in the Holy of Holies.

THE SIGN OF THE SON OF MAN IN HEAVEN
(MATTHEW 24:30)

THE NAME: For the Advent of Joshua is "the land" (Leland), for the iniquity of Joshua (Zech. 3:4) and the iniquity of "the land" (Zech. 3:9) is the same iniquity, the dirty garment (Zech. 3:3,4).[11]

THE ADDRESS: For the Advent of Joshua is the "stone with seven eyes" (Zech 3:9) which is located in the mountains of the northwest (Isaiah 49:12). It is just about halfway between the two largest mountains of brass or copper in the world, Lincoln and Butte Montana (Zech. 6:1), of which "the four spirits of the heavens, which go forth from standing before the LORD of all the earth" (Zech. 6:5).

THE DATE: For the Advent of Joshua is 1963 A.D. as given by the prophet Daniel 12:12, and the 100 Granite Blocks lining the Holy of Holies, when he stood before angel of the Lord and satan was at his right hand to oppose him. And His Proclamation on April 29th, 1971, with the "stone with seven eyes" before him, indicated by the 108 Granite Blocks overlaying the floor of the Holy of Holies and the 9 Granite Beams forming the ceiling of the Holy of Holies.

THE PROFESSION: of Joshua is to establish in the world the "Twin institutions" (The Universal House of Justice and the Guardianship) of the Branch — 'Abdu'l-Baha (Zech. 3:8).

THE PIT

The bottomless pit is the pit of error, and is the way of the world. It represents the end: The Great Catastrophe!

THE COFFER

The Coffer that is found in the King's Chamber (Holy of Holies) is the only movable piece of furniture in the Pyramid and is of the utmost importance. It is of the same cubic capacity as the Ark of the Covenant of Moses that he placed in the Tabernacle in the desert and was later placed in the Temple of Solomon, which has been lost for over 2500 years, making the Jews apostate. It occurs at the place (in the chronological time-scale) of Baha'u'llah's penning of the Book of His Covenant, the *Kitab-i-Ahd*, at the Holy Shrine of Bahji where God made Baha'u'llah's permanent home in the Holy Land in September of 1879, (thus, the re-establishment of Israel). It also occurs exactly 6000 years from the birth of Adam and his leaving the Fertile Crescent (The Garden of Eden), for the land between the rivers, (Ur, or Babylon),

---

11   "iniquity — unevenness, inequality, injustice, from iniquus: unequal", cf. *Webster's New Universal Unabridged Dictionary*. One of the meanings of the word "iniquity" is injustice. This iniquity and injustice was the miscarriage of justice — in an unjust legal system — that put me in prison.

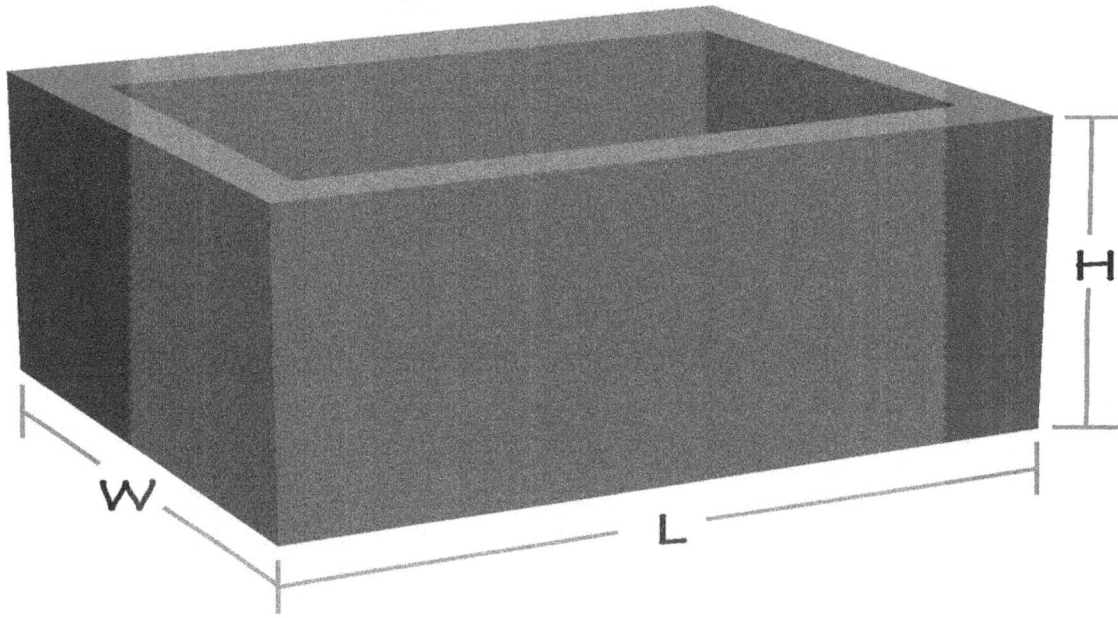

VOLUME
$41.2132(H) \times 38.7534(W) \times 90.1604(L) = 144{,}000$

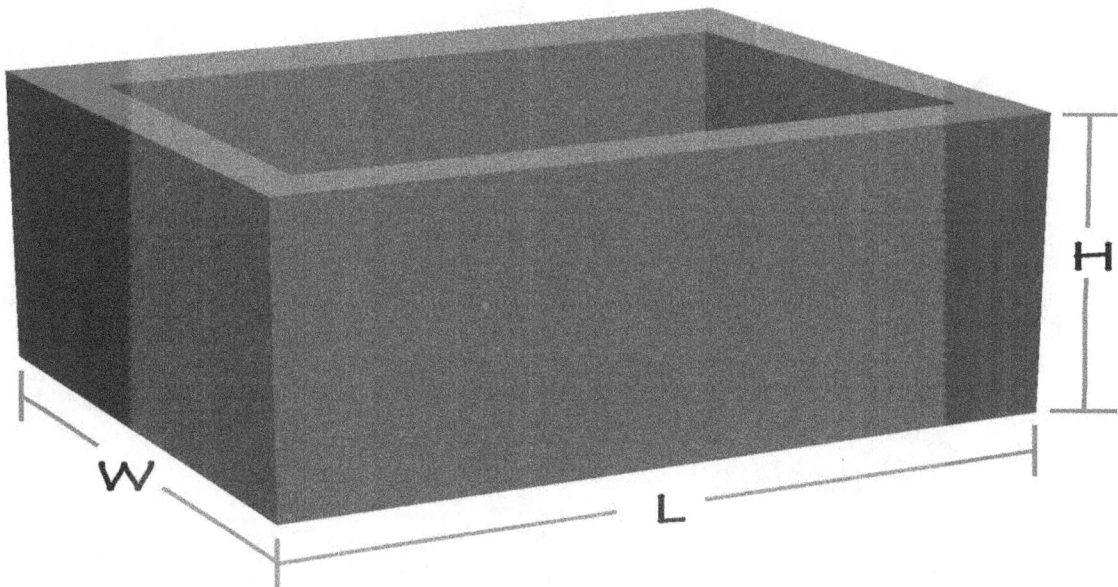

$144{,}000(W \times H \times L) \times 13 = 1{,}872{,}000$

$1{,}872{,}000 \div 365.242465 = 5125.36240823$

King's Chamber

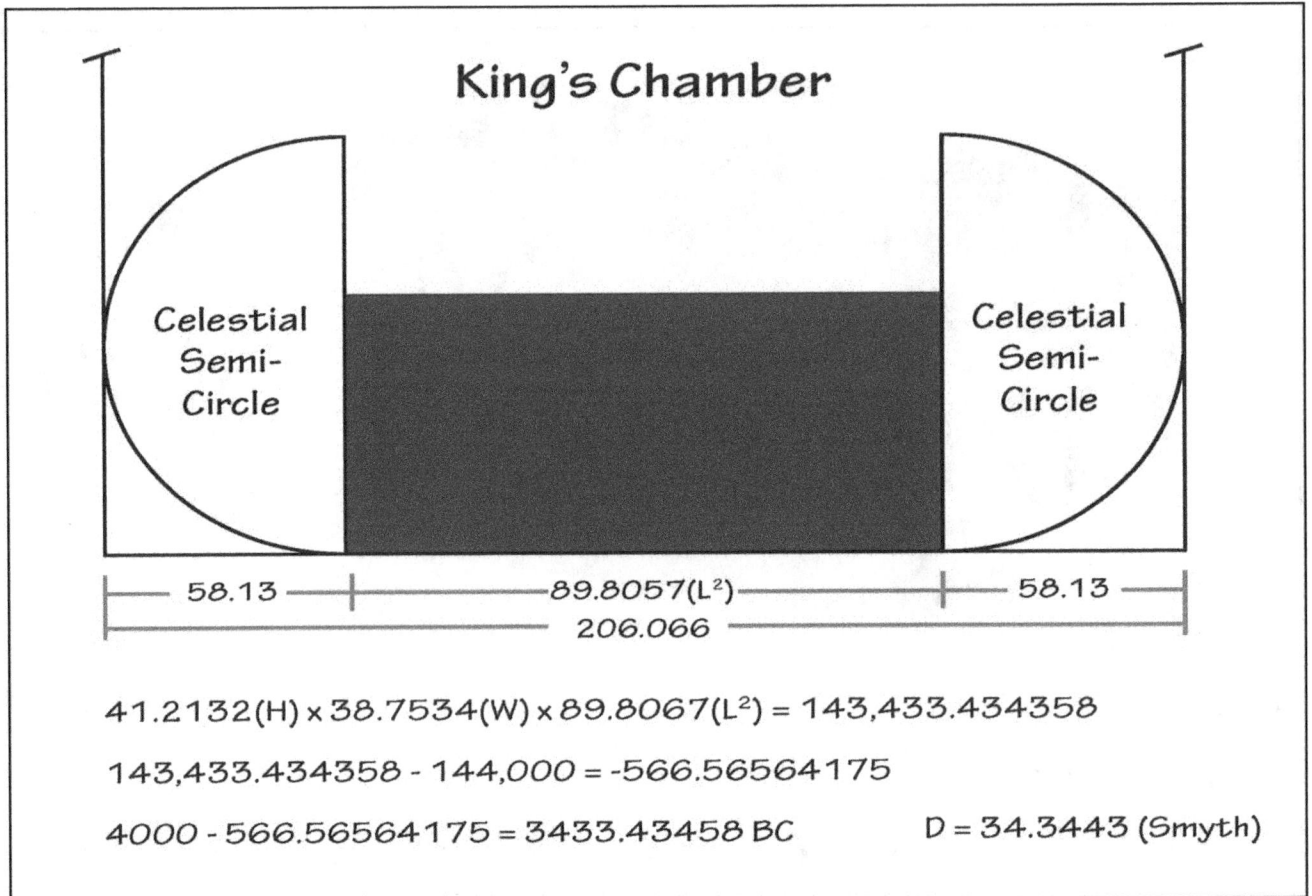

58.13 —— $89.8057(L^2)$ —— 58.13

206.066

$41.2132(H) \times 38.7534(W) \times 89.8067(L^2) = 143{,}433.434358$

$143{,}433.434358 - 144{,}000 = -566.56564175$

$4000 - 566.56564175 = 3433.43458 \text{ BC}$ $D = 34.3443 \text{ (Smyth)}$

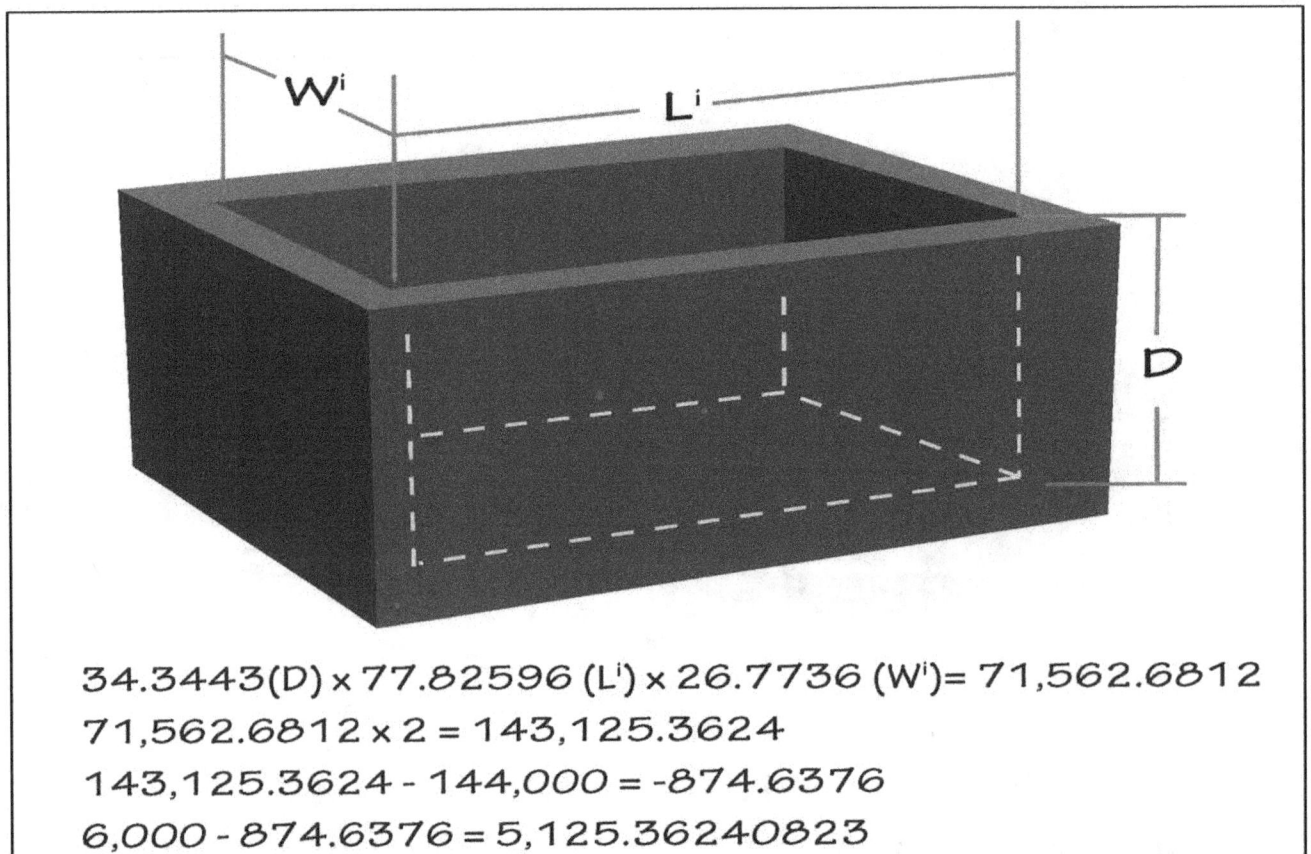

$34.3443(D) \times 77.82596\ (L^i) \times 26.7736\ (W^i) = 71{,}562.6812$

$71{,}562.6812 \times 2 = 143{,}125.3624$

$143{,}125.3624 - 144{,}000 = -874.6376$

$6{,}000 - 874.6376 = 5{,}125.36240823$

1878.681 + 4121.319 = 6000 years. It is placed on the center line of the Pyramid, thus the re-establishing of mankind to Paradise (the Kingdom of God on earth). It is through the Covenant of Baha'u'llah that mankind is to become permanently united and remain so. This is represented in the Great Pyramid by the entrance opening (on the north slope of the Pyramid), and all of the Passage-ways and Chambers are 286.1022 Pyramid inches to the left of the center line. Being left of center is represented by six work days of a thousand years each, (see 2 Peter 3:8), thus bringing us to the Sabbath of a thousand years of peace (Rev. 20:2, 13). Moses when he was on earth was the Temple of God (Manifestation of God). He transferred from himself his teachings, laws and ordinances to the Ark of the Covenant, and placed the Book of his Covenant on top and placed it in the Holy of Holies in the Tabernacle. The High Priest only was allowed to enter the Holy of Holies and then only once a year (that is, for the Day of Atonement). Here he whispered the Tetragrammation YHWH atoning for the sins of Israel. This Tabernacle (Temple) replaced the Manifestation as being the intermediary between God and man. With the Advent of Baha'u'llah we have the return of the Temple (Manifestation of God) and His Covenant, with the Advent of the High Priest (Joshua), Israel (God's Chosen) is re-established in the world (Rev. 11:19).

THE CAP STONE

The Guardianship of the Baha'i Faith is the Promised Zerubbabel, the governor of the New Jerusalem (Rev. 21:2, Haggai 1:1). He is that Great King that is seated upon the throne, that brings forth the CAP STONE, AMID SHOUTS OF GRACE GRACE TO IT!!! (Zech. 4:7). The Cap Stone represents the Kingdom Of God on earth as it is in heaven, of which the Guardian is the sine qua non. This is the stone that the builders rejected, the corner stone of the Kingdom of God on earth is the Guardianship, for it is the head of the corner itself (Psalms 118:22, Matthew 21:42, Mark 12:10). The Guardianship is the righteous Branch (Jeremiah 23:5, Zech. 3:8). He is the executive branch of the Universal House of Justice. The executive branch along with the legislative branch comprise the Universal House of Justice which is freed from all error and where by this body all the difficult problems are to be resolved (*Will and Testament of 'Abdu'l-Baha*, pp. 14-15). The "Hands" of the Cause appointed by Shoghi Effendi seized authority of the Faith after his death in 1957. Led by Ruhiyyih Khanum they (the "Hands") did away with Shoghi Effendi's appointed son (first International Baha'i Council) and elected a bogus UHJ in 1963 when they had no authority to do so. After Shoghi Effendi died, his Hands died as well. They had no authority. This bogus House of the Lord lies in ruins — the bogus Universal House of Justice — for the builders of that House, the sans guardian Baha'is (covenant-breaking "Hands"), rejected the Guardian, the Branch, the Corner Stone (Haggai 1:4). Therefore there will be a second reassembling of the Tribes of Israel (Isaiah 11:11).

The first reassembling was completed under Shoghi Effendi, when he had the message of the Kingdom brought to every part of the globe (Matthew 24:14), where his administration became the Baha'i establishment. But the covenant-breaking "Hands" did away with his plan and their bogus UHJ has now fallen and has become the seventh Head of the Beast. Shoghi Effendi himself said that his administration could fall and another be raised up in its stead. Therefore, the "Hands faith," which is the apostate Baha'i faith should be considered as the seventh king, or dynasty, of Rev. 17:10. Thus those that bind themselves to that administration set up by the covenant-breaking "Hands" have neither the Baha'i Faith nor the Guardianship, but are apostate and are for the fire along with the Beast and its six other Heads.

BAHA'I IS THE NEW NAME FOR ISRAEL, WHICH MEANS OF GLORY (ISAIAH 62:2, REV. 3:12, ISAIAH 6:3, EZEKIEL 43:2))

Israel, which means "God's Chosen" or "the Elect", at the death of Solomon split into Israel with the ten northern tribes forming the Northern Kingdom, and Judah, the two southern tribes forming the Southern Kingdom. This started the condition of the "curse" of Deuteronomy 28:15-68. Then several centuries later, in 721 B.C., still under the conditions of the curse, the Northern Kingdom, Israel, went into captivity into Assyria, and became known as the "ten lost tribes of Israel". In 606 B.C., Judah went into captivity into Babylon, but still under the conditions of the curse — for they had lost the Ark of the Covenant — part of Judah returned to Jerusalem seventy years later, in 536 B.C., to rebuild their Temple. More returned in 457 B.C. to rebuild their city, but their city and Temple were again destroyed and the remnant of Jews that survived were dispersed right after their rejection of their Messiah by Titus at the head of the Roman legions in 70 A.D. (Deut. 28:36,64).

Israel, under its new name Baha'i — of Glory (Isaiah 62:2, Rev. 3:15, Isaiah 6:3, Ezekiel 43:2) — did not come out of captivity and become regathered from the four corners of the earth until the coming of the Bab and Baha'u'llah. The Bab made his declaration in that part of ancient Babylon where the tribe of Judah went into captivity. This declaration was exactly 2300 years (1844 A.D.) from the order to restore and rebuild Jerusalem in 457 B.C. (Daniel 8:14). Baha'u'llah, Who was of the Tribe of Judah, was exiled from Tehran, Iran to Baghdad, Iraq. Iraq was that part of the ancient Assyrian Empire where Israel went into captivity and where Baha'u'llah made His Proclamation in 1863. His Revelation was of the potency of the Holy of Holies and His Covenant establishes the Ark of the Covenant in the Holy of Holies, which establishes the Davidic Kingship in the institution of the Guardianship of the Faith and the executive branch of the UHJ; and also establishes the legislative branch of the UHJ, which represents the Covenant passed down from Abraham through Joseph for the multitude of nations (rod of iron). The Davidic Kingship is the part of Abraham's Covenant passed down through Judah (rod of wood). This Covenant comes together (wood + iron = Gold) with its new name Baha'i (Glory).[12] Baha'u'llah brought a government whereby justice will be established in the world for all peoples, with a Universal House of Justice (rod of Gold). This UHJ is now in existence in its first stage as the second International Baha'i Council established Jan. 9, 1991 by the Promised Joshua (Jesus) — the High Priest — now standing in the Holy of Holies regathering Israel on its second gathering (Isaiah 11:11).

The first gathering of Israel (Deut. 30:1-10) was completed during Shoghi Effendi's "Ten Year World Crusade" in which the Baha'i Faith was established throughout the world. Israel was dispersed throughout the world in 1960 when the Baha'is under the direction of the covenant-breaking "Hands" rejected the Second Guardian of the Baha'i Faith, Mason Remey, and

---

12   See Ezekiel Chapter 37 and *Selections from the Writings of 'Abdu'l-Baha* (# 142), pp. 165-167, for the prophecy and a brief explanation of the joining of the two rods (wood and iron) into one single rod (gold) of the everlasting Covenant.

THE GREAT PYRAMID'S ASTRONOMICAL CHRONOGRAPH AND GEOMETRICAL EPHEMERIS.

FRAMEWORK FOR GEOMETRICAL DEFINITION OF ASTRONOMICAL FORMULAE FOR PRECESSIONAL AND PERIHELION MOTION AND VARIATIONS.

FIG. A.

9-21-2001

As defined and confirmed by the Pyramid's various and independent astronomical formulæ and their integrated angular values: (1) o A.P.=Autumnal Equinox 4000 B.C.; (2) 3000 A.P.=Autumnal Equinox 1000 B.C.; and (3) 6000 A.P.=Autumnal Equinox 2001 A.D.

NOTE.—A.P. denotes *Anno Pyr.*

September 21, 2001 A.D.

AUTUMNAL EQUINOX
SEPTEMBER 21st
FALL 2001 AD

CAPSTONE VOLUME
2520 CUBIC CUBITS
7 X 360 = 2520
("SEVEN TIMES" DANIEL 7:25)
2520 YEARS

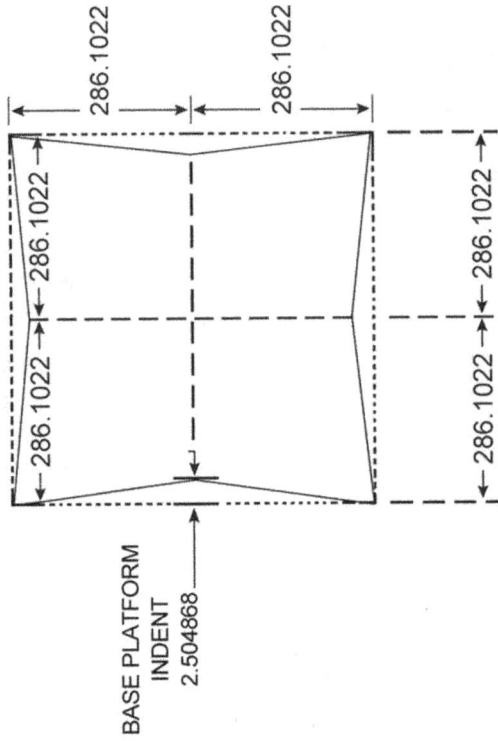

APOTHEM DEPTH
OF FOUR FACES
AT CAPSTONE BASE
2.748267

286.1022

286.1022 | 286.1022

APOTHEM CREASE

$$\begin{array}{r} 2544.441628 \text{ cc} \\ -\ 24.441628 \text{ cc} \\ \hline = 2520.000000 \text{ cc} \\ = 2520 \text{ YEARS} \end{array}$$

"For, Behold,
I will bring forth my servant
the BRANCH."
(Zech. 3:8 KJV)

"He will bring out
THE CAPSTONE
accompanied by shouts of:
'Grace, grace to it!'"
(Zech. 4:7 HCSB)

PYRAMID TOP PLATFORM AREA
519. 2821 SQUARE CUBITS
SEPTEMBER 21, 520 BC

286.1022

286.1022

286.1022

286.1022

286.1022

286.1022

CENTER LINE

BASE PLATFORM
INDENT
2.504868

"When the **foundation** of the LORD's Temple
was laid [September 21, 520 BC]. Pay attention!"
"From **this very day** I will bless you." (Hag. 2:18,19 ISV)

519.2821 BC + 2520 YEARS = 2000.7179 AD: **SEPTEMBER 21, 2001 AD**

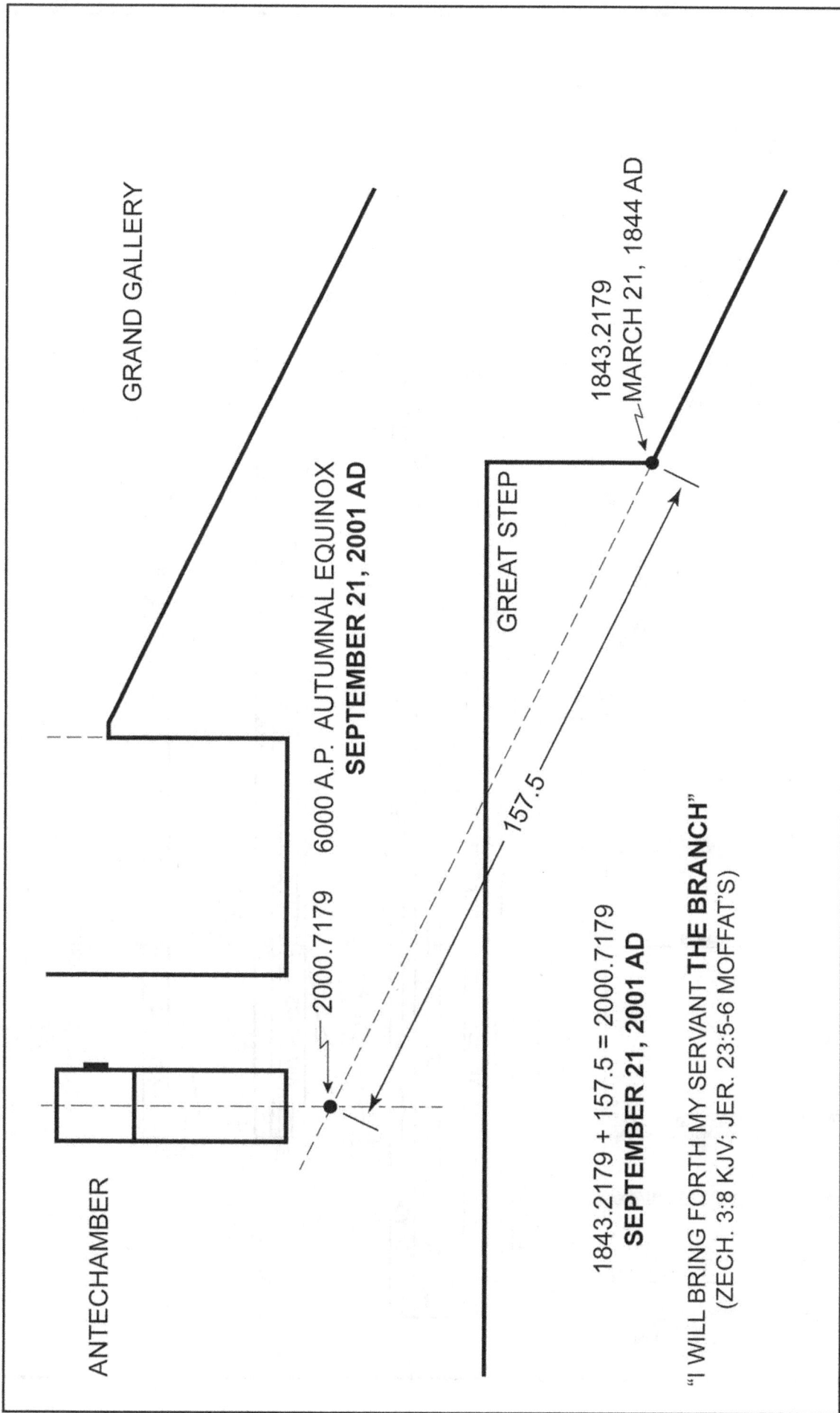

GRAND GALLERY

ANTECHAMBER

2000.7179   6000 A.P.   AUTUMNAL EQUINOX
SEPTEMBER 21, 2001 AD

157.5

GREAT STEP

1843.2179
MARCH 21, 1844 AD

1843.2179 + 157.5 = 2000.7179
SEPTEMBER 21, 2001 AD

"I WILL BRING FORTH MY SERVANT **THE BRANCH**"
(ZECH. 3:8 KJV; JER. 23:5-6 MOFFAT'S)

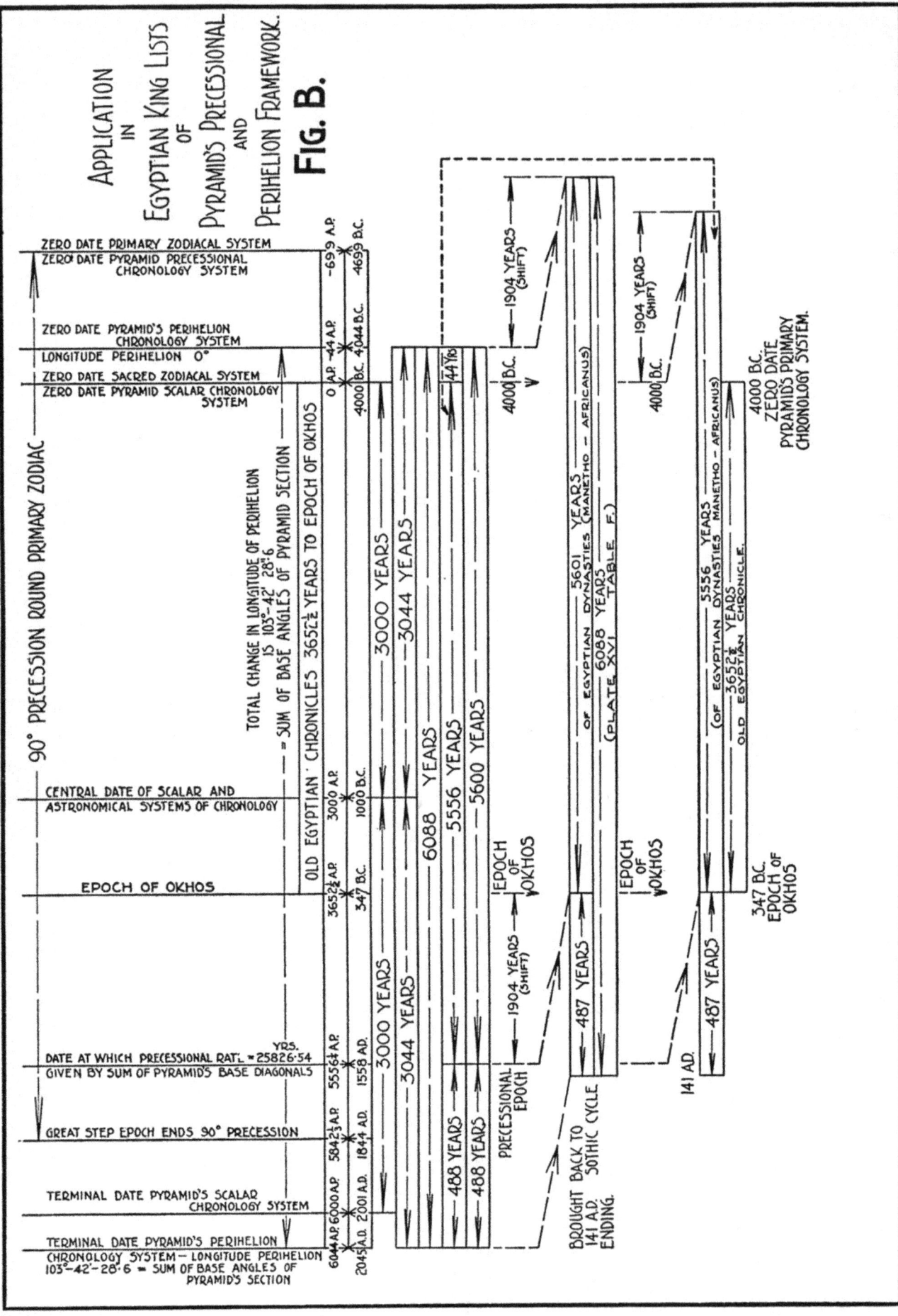

TERMINAL DATE PYRAMID'S SCALAR CHRONOLOGY SYSTEM AUTUMNAL EQUINOX (Sept., 21) 2001 A.D.

APPLICATION IN EGYPTIAN KING LISTS OF PYRAMID'S PRECESSIONAL AND PERIHELION FRAMEWORK. FIG. B.

90° PRECESSION ROUND PRIMARY ZODIAC

ZERO DATE PRIMARY ZODIACAL SYSTEM
ZERO DATE PYRAMID PRECESSIONAL CHRONOLOGY SYSTEM
ZERO DATE PYRAMID'S PERIHELION CHRONOLOGY SYSTEM
LONGITUDE PERIHELION 0°
ZERO DATE SACRED ZODIACAL SYSTEM
ZERO DATE PYRAMID SCALAR CHRONOLOGY SYSTEM

TOTAL CHANGE IN LONGITUDE OF PERIHELION IS 103°-42'-28".6 = SUM OF BASE ANGLES OF PYRAMID SECTION

OLD EGYPTIAN CHRONICLES 3652¼ YEARS TO EPOCH OF OKHOS

CENTRAL DATE OF SCALAR AND ASTRONOMICAL SYSTEMS OF CHRONOLOGY

EPOCH OF OKHOS

DATE AT WHICH PRECESSIONAL RATE = 25826·54 YRS. GIVEN BY SUM OF PYRAMID'S BASE DIAGONALS

GREAT STEP EPOCH ENDS 90° PRECESSION

TERMINAL DATE PYRAMID'S SCALAR CHRONOLOGY SYSTEM

TERMINAL DATE PYRAMID'S PERIHELION CHRONOLOGY SYSTEM — LONGITUDE PERIHELION 103°-42'-28".6 = SUM OF BASE ANGLES OF PYRAMID'S SECTION

-69·9 A.P.   4699 B.C.
0 A.P. -44 A.P.   4000 B.C. 4044 B.C.
3000 A.P.   1000 B.C.
3652¼ A.P.   347 B.C.
5556¼ A.P.   1558 A.D.
5842¾ A.P.   1844 A.D.
6000 A.P.   2001 A.D.
6044 A.P.   2045 A.D.

3000 YEARS
3044 YEARS
6088 YEARS
5556 YEARS
5600 YEARS
44 YRS.

3000 YEARS
3044 YEARS
488 YEARS
488 YEARS

1904 YEARS (SHIFT)
4000 B.C.

EPOCH OF OKHOS
5601 YEARS (OF EGYPTIAN DYNASTIES — AFRICANUS) 6088 YEARS (PLATE XVI TABLE F.)
487 YEARS
BROUGHT BACK TO SOTHIC CYCLE 141 A.D. ENDING.
EPOCH OF OKHOS
1904 YEARS (SHIFT)

1904 YEARS (SHIFT)
4000 B.C.

5556 YEARS (OF EGYPTIAN DYNASTIES MANETHO — AFRICANUS)
3652¼ YEARS OLD EGYPTIAN CHRONICLE.
4000 B.C. ZERO DATE PYRAMID'S PRIMARY CHRONOLOGY SYSTEM.
347 B.C. EPOCH OF OKHOS

141 A.D.
487 YEARS

PRECESSIONAL EPOCH
1904 YEARS (SHIFT)

The Pyramid chronology of the Egyptian King Lists, and its application in the King Lists, confirm the chronology as derived from the Pyramid's astronomical formula. The King Lists independently prove that o A.P. = Autumnal Equinox 4000 B.C. and 6000 A.P. = Autumnal Equinox 2001 A.D.

the First Guardian's plan for the first International Baha'i Council to become a World Court in 1963, for a plan of their own to set up in its stead a headless-monster form of the UHJ, causing the second Guardian to expel them and their apostate administration from the Baha'i Religious Faith.

On the very same date that the first gathering of Israel commenced, March 21, 1844, which is the start of the Baha'i Era and calendar, the Sultan of Turkey, who then ruled Palestine, made a decree that the Jew — apostate Judah — could again live in Jerusalem. This annulled a decree made by Omar in the seventh century that prohibited Jews from living there. In the same year (1868 A.D.) that Baha'u'llah as a prisoner of the Turkish Empire brought the twelve tribes of Israel out of Baghdad to the Valley of Sharon and Mt. Carmel (Ezekiel 43:1-7, Isaiah 35:1,2) the Sultan made another decree that the Jews could now buy and own land in Jerusalem.[13] The Jews now have an independent nation there called the State of Israel. They know that they are apostate, however, for they do not have their Temple worship as prescribed by Moses. They would like to rebuild their Temple on Mt. Moriah, where Solomon built the first one, but the Aqsa Mosque has been built over the site, and their Holy of Holies is buried underneath it. If they should somehow be able to destroy the mosque (such an act would bring on World War Three) and rebuild their Temple, they would still be apostate, for the Ark of their Covenant became lost in Babylon and has never been found. Even if they had the Ark, they still have no High Priest, because several hundred years after the second destruction of their Temple and their dispersion, the High Priesthood came to an end. This is of the utmost importance, for only a High Priest can enter the Holy of Holies, for without a High Priest in the Holy of Holies to officiate before the Ark of the Covenant the Jew has no intermediary between them and God. Moses when he was on earth was the intermediary between Israel and God. Before he died, he transferred this intermediaryship to the Temple (Tabernacle). The Jews only one solution to their dilemma is to accept the new Temple —the Bab and Baha'u'llah — and the Advent of the High Priest, Joshua (Jesus), who is now standing in the Holy of Holies before the Ark of the Covenant that are sent them by God.

ZERUBBABEL AND JOSHUA

The Guardianship of the Baha'i Faith (executive branch) and the body, or the legislative branch of the UHJ, will be established with my assistance; this "House" of the Lord — Universal House of Justice — will be built (Haggai 1:1), on Mt. Carmel — God's Holy Mountain — in the country of Israel (Rev. 21:10, Isaiah 2:2, 3, 4, 11:1-9). Because I fulfill the prophecies for the Promised Joshua (return of Jesus), I therefore am that servant who is to bring Jacob back to God, so that Israel might be gathered unto Him (Isaiah 49:5,6, 27:12, 10:20-24), for this stone wall that has seven eyes is continually before the sight of God (Isaiah 49:16).

As Joshua of old took the twelve tribes of Israel across the River Jordan into the Promised Land, and conquered the seven Kingdoms of Palestine, I, the Promised Joshua for our day, when accompanied by the other Knight of the Lord, Dr. Opal M. Jensen who also remained

---

13   This Decree commonly known as The Edict of Toleration, dated March 21, 1844, by the Sublime Porte (the Sultan of Turkey), and the subsequent Decree of 1868, allowing the Jews to both buy and own land in Jerusalem, are both still extant and available as a matter of public record.

firm and steadfast in the Covenant; and assisted by His grace from on high, strengthened by faith, aided by the power of understanding, and reinforced by the Legions of the Covenant, who are the twelve tribes of Israel on the second and last gathering; the 144,000, the Elect, the Chosen, the Virgins; will arise and slay the remnant of the seven headed Beast (Rev. 7:9,14). These are the 1/3 that are left alive, that had been put into the fire and refined as silver is refined. They will call on the name of God (Rev. 2:17) and He will answer them (Zech. 13:9). We will set up the "Kingdom of God on Earth", by rejecting the bogus UHJ set up by those covenant-breaking "Hands," and by crossing the River Jordan into acceptance of God's Plan, by establishing the Universal House of Justice on Mt. Carmel, with the Guardian of the Cause of God seated upon the Throne!

The Virgins (Rev. 14:4) are those who have their past ways forgiven, by accepting **the everlasting Covenant**, the Covenant of Baha'u'llah (*Kitab-i-Ahd*), and come under the guidance of the Universal House of Justice (sIBC). ALL OTHERS ARE BEAST WORSHIPPERS AND ARE STILL IN THEIR SINS AND ARE FOR THE FIRE!!! (Rev. 13:4, 8, Isaiah 24:5,6).

REFLECT! CONSIDER! O PEOPLE OF ERROR!

AFTERWORD
–Neal Chase–

The final vision in the Book of Revelation corresponds to the final prophesied act depicted in the Great Pyramid Prophecy: that is the placing of the capstone upon the top of the pyramid. This is spoken of in the Bible and the Book of Revelation and many have written of this pre-eminent event in relation the completion of the 6000 years prophetical cycle of Adam depicted in the Great pyramid prophecy that culminates the final appearance of the last promised one of the Adamic Cycle in 2001 AD who is also the first promised one of the Newly inaugurated 5000 Century Baha'i Cycle for the creation of the "Oneness of Humanity" whose watchword shall be "unity in diversity." Of this Capstone Dr. Leland Jensen writes:

I have a mandate--to bring forth and establish the BRANCH--I must and I will accomplish this. NOTHING IN HEAVEN OR ON EARTH CAN PREVENT ME IN DOING THIS.

The Guardianship of the Baha'i Faith is the promised Zerubbabel, the govemor of the New Jerusalem (Rev. 21:2, Haggai 1:1) he is that Great King that is seated upon the throne, that brings forth the CAP STONE, AMID SHOUTS OF GRACE GRACE TO IT!!! (Zech. 4:7) The Cap Stone represents the Kingdom of God on earth as it is in heaven, of which the Guardian is the sine qua non. This is the stone (the guardian the living Christ of the Baha'i world order) that the builders have rejected, the corner stone of the kingdom of God on earth is the Guardianship, for it is the head of the corner itself (Psalms 118:22, Matthew 21:42, Mark 12:10). (Dr. Leland Jensen, *The Beast: Is About to Be Dead!*)

Thus the date for the coming forth and establishment of the guardianship (throne of King David) through the appearance of the person of the living descendant of King David through Baha'u'llah and 'Abdu'l-Baha is the prophesied date of September 21st 2001 AD that is given as the Terminal Date of the time scale in David Davidson's book *The Great Pyramid Its Divine Message*, pages 359-368. This is depicted as the prophesied 2520 years--the "Seven Times" of the great vision of Daniel chapter 4--added to September 21st, 520 BC that brings us to September 21st, 2001 AD. This same date is included in the volume measure of the Capstone which is 2520 cubic cubits representing the 2520 prophesied years. The top truncated platform measures is 520 square cubits representing the prophesied foundation date of the Laying of the Comer-Stone of the second temple on September 21st, 520 BC. The date of September 21st, 520 BC plus 2520 years is September 21st 2001 AD. Thus God brought forth myself, Neal Chase (the great grandson of 'Abdu'l-Baha) as His "servant, the BRANCH" (Zech 3:8 KJV) during the prophesied "ten days" period from 9-11, 2001 AD to public projection on September 21st, 2001 AD in the fulfillment of prophecy that--although with Our foreknowledge of the date of the 9-11--occurred against my will.

After that is was later discovered that the exact day of September 21st, 2001 AD was given in the Pyramid and other scriptures for the coming forth of the Branch. So it is written that "every body shall bow" and "every knee shall bend" as we align our will with the will of God and in the words of Christ who was obedient unto death: "Not my will O Lord, but Thine!"

EPILOGUE 1999:

GEORGE WILLIAMS PROPHESIES THE RETURN OF JESUS IN DEER LODGE, MONTANA!

Sheriff Burton charged his horse forward in a mighty spree to run Joseph Morris into the ground! Morris stood calm and grabbed the horse by its bridle causing the horse to buck back on its haunches. Burton fired his gun killing Morris on the spot.
—Eyewitness Account, Morrisite Massacre, Utah, 1862.

From one of the most important books ever written, *For Christ Will Come Tomorrow: Joseph Morris and the Saga of the Morrisites*, by C. LeRoy Anderson, (and the original source material archive in Logan, Utah) we read of the heroic death of Joseph Morris and the slaughter of the Morrisites in 1862 climaxing in the clear and vibrant prophecies of the prophet George Willams in 1863, who fearlessly and openly announced that by the will and plan of Almighty God, the return of Jesus would take place in Deer Lodge, Montana in a special building (temple-prison) to be built expressly for that divinely ordained purpose from the stone of the surrounding mountains. This amazing testimony prophetically announced over 100 years ago corresponds simultaneously with the outpouring of the Revelation of Baha'u'llah proclaimed at the same exact time in April of 1863 from the Garden of Ridvan (paradise) on the entire other side of the world!

Completely unknown to the Baha'i Faith and to Dr. Leland Jensen, it was not until 1990, 19 years after the proclamation Dr. Jensen, and the initial publication of "THE BEAST" in 1971, that these amazing prophecies and the incredible story of the Morrisite Massacre came to light. The fact that these things were entirely unknown to Dr. Jensen at the time of his proclamation when he had "the stone with seven eyes" before him in 1971, is witnessed especially by, Dr. Anderson and Dr. Balch of the University of Montana, who were conducting different studies though at the same time in the field of Social Sciences, as well as Professor Domitriovich of Kootenai College, and Neal Chase, board member of the second International Baha'i Council.

You may have heard of a termite or a parasite, but what in the world is a Morrisite? In the late 1850's, early 1860's, Joseph Morris rose up as a Mormon reformer much like Martin Luther that tried to reform the Catholic church and the papacy. Unlike Martin Luther who had eight German princes to protect him, Joseph Morris was murdered by Sheriff Burton under the direct orders of Brigham Young in 1862. The people who rejected the corruption of Brigham Young at that time of the great Morrisite Massacre, were named after Morris and called Morrisites. In 1863, at the same time as Baha'u'llah's proclamation outside of Baghdad, Iraq, George WILLIAMS who was never a Morrisite, received a vision that corresponds absolutely with the Bible prophecy that the return of Jesus would occur later in the Deer Lodge Valley in Montana. This message revitalized the Morrisites survivors who then exodused the Utah territory under the protection and military escort of General Connor, by the direct orders of then President,

Abraham Lincoln, of the United States of America. Infuriated Young sent out "avenging angels" to kill and wipe out the Morrisites, and try to kill Williams who he couldn't find because he was using a code-name "the prophet Cainan" (for safety reasons) and periodically changed his mailing address.

Williams prophesied that the return of Jesus would be put in prison wearing a dirty garment that would later be removed corresponding to Zech. Chapter 3.[14] He stated that this Jesus would be the High Priest after the order of the Melchizedek[15] (see Hebrews 5, 6 and 7), and not the return of Christ, which was fulfilled prophetically by Baha'u'llah, that great descendant of King David, the Universal Manifestation of God anointed by God directly with the Holy Spirit. Williams also prophesied that the return of Jesus in Deer Lodge[16] would come to establish the global government of the Kingdom of God on earth as it is in heaven[17] and that this Jesus would explain all the hidden meaning in the Great Pyramid of Giza[18] which in fact Leland did do while he had the "stone with seven eyes before him."

Williams said he also saw that this personage would likewise fulfill Bible prophecy and be a direct descendant of the King of Denmark, which Dr. Jensen is.[19] He also stated that he saw the new name "Leland" but refused to tell the people of it for a wisdom of God.[20] Williams sent a messenger all the way around the world to rebuke the sultan of Turkey for imprisoning Baha'u'llah, heard the angels singing His name (The Greatest Name) and prophesied the fall of the Ottoman empire (the dragon) in World War I, years before it took place.[21] Even greater, Williams gave the Morrisite leadership here in America explicit instructions to disband the group on August 9th of 1969, which would be the date that they would be able to meet the return of Jesus in Deer Lodge.[22] August 9th, 1969 was the first full day, that Dr. Leland Jensen began his ministry in Deer Lodge when against his will, God placed the "stone with seven eyes" before him on that day (August 9th, 1969) in fulfillment of both Morrisite and Bible prophecy!

That these are the true facts is a matter of public record. God never makes a promise but that He keeps it. A prophecy is a promise, and these have all been fulfilled — these and much, much more! These things can also be read in the book *Ezekiel's Temple in Montana*, which shows that "this stone with seven eyes" fulfills Bible as well as Morrisite prophecy for the seven towered temple depicted by Ezekiel in the last nine chapters of his book, where the return of Jesus is to be; and also the book *OVER THE WALL*, which gives the proofs and evidences of these things in a clear and easy way.

---

14   Williams, *The High Priesthoods Return* (1870), and "Letter to Rasmusson," (April, 1873).

15   Williams, "Letter to Erasmussen," (December 27, 1881).

16   Williams, "Letter to My dear Saint James and John, G.S.L." (August 9, 1865); "Letter to Dear Sis Thomas," (July, 24, 1873); "Letter from Williams," (June 13, 1880), cf. Anderson, page 114; also, Anderson, pp. 222-223.

17   Williams, "Letter to My Dear Bro. James," (1879).

18   Williams, "Letter to Erasmussen," (December 27, 1881).

19   Williams, "Letter to Rasmusson," (April, 1873).

20   ibid.

21   Williams, *Vision of Muhammad* (1867).

22   MCLU, 2:2, and (MCLU) index book. Morrisitie Collection: Marie-Eccles Caine Archive, Logan, Utah, at the Utah State University.

THE BIBLE PROPHESIES THE RETURN OF JESUS TO BE IN PRISON

In the Bible where it prophesies the return of Jesus at the time of the final judgment, (see Matt. 25 — the prophecy for his second coming), Jesus himself prophesies that when he returns on the second coming he will be naked, hungry, sick and a stranger in prison. Dr. Leland Jensen was naked when they took him by force, and against his will, took off all his nice clothes and dressed him in dirty prison clothes. He went hungry when he was in that prison because being a doctor of natural medicine he was used to eating raw foods, fruits and vegetables and all they gave was red-meat, potatoes, white bread and coffee They found him to be so sick when he was in that prison that they sent him to Galen State Pulmonary Institute. And Dr. Leland Jensen was a stranger in that prison, because he was a stranger to the Christians, who are looking for a mythical "Jesus" to come come floating down out of the sky on a cloud. "Blessed are the sheep (those on the right hand) for when I was naked, hungry, sick and a stranger in prison you came and visited me" and "he say also unto them on the left hand, Depart from me, ye cursed, into everlasting fire [thermonuclear] prepared for the devil and his angels: for when I was an hungered, and ye gave me no meat: I was thirsty and ye gave me no drink, I was a stranger, and ye took me not in: naked and ye clothed me not: sick and in prison, and ye visited me not...Verily I say unto you, Inasmuch as ye did it not to one of the least of these [Jesus and his fellow inmates], ye did it not to me. And these shall go away into everlasting punishment: but the righteous into life eternal" (Matt. 25:43-46).

*"Be not forgetful to entertain **strangers**: for thereby some have entertained **angels** unawares. Remember them that are in **prison**..."* — St. Paul, Book of Hebrews 13:1.

THE SILVER STATE PO

103rd Year – No. 49   DEER LODGE, POWELL COUNTY, MONTANA 59722

"I told him to wait until the 29th, because that's when we're supposed to have the second coming of Jesus," Sheriff Fiske said, referring to a small faction in Deer Lodge who have predicted Jesus will soon return at the city's Old Montana State Prison. "I told him he could get two for one," Fiske joked.

April 18, 1991

M.S.P.

Bigfoot captured!

capture of Bigfoot. Some people can't be convinced there is no   pretty ganted up. Mine's a lot meaner - he never eats fruit and

THE RAPTURE IS NOW

Jesus has just returned! He has come a second time, and already a number of the dead in Christ have resurrected out of their graves and have met him in the air, the air is down here on earth, the higher up you go the less air there is. This is just like it says in the Bible. He has "descended from heaven with a cry of command, with the archangel's call, and with the sound of the trumpet of God" (I Thess. 4:16). Those that have been left alive are about to join them and meet him in the air (I Thess. 4:17). Their number will increase until they comprise the 144,000 of Revelation, chapters 7 and 14, of whom will be the elect of Matt 24:22. Then the bombs will drop! The multitude will not resurrect until the bombs drop on their churches (tombs) destroying them. "These are they who" will "have come out of great tribulation" — the four winds of destruction — (Rev. 7:14). By the end of this century the four great waves of destruction, that will come one succeeding the other, will be over. Before this happens "every eye will see him" (Rev. 1:7), and every head will bow before the Throne (Rev. 7:9-12). This will comprise those that are left, that had not been taken by the great catastrophe. He is now here upon the earth alive breathing air, not up in the sky where there is not any air.

Most of the Christians will miss the rapture before the bombs drop on their cities because they are so dead in the theologies (clouds of heaven) of their church that they will not be able to see him on his return until they have become purified by the fire of the oncoming thermo-nuclear holocaust, or one of the other succeeding waves to the great tribulation. As a cloud in the sky veils the light of the sun, so a cloud of heaven veils the light of Jesus on his return.

Because of these theologies the Christians — the dead in Christ — believe that Jesus resurrected up into the sky, and that when he returns the rapture will take place in the sky, yet no place in the scriptures does it say this. They are like the Jews of 2000 years ago that had murdered their Messiah. They had the prophecy for the return of Elijah before the coming of their Messiah — Christ — (Malachi 4:5).

Like Jesus, Elijah had ascended up into heaven: "And it came to pass, as they still went on, and talked, that behold, there appeared a chariot of fire, and horses of fire, and parted them both asunder; and Elijah went up by a whirlwind into heaven" (II Kings 2:11). The Jews at the time of Jesus did not know the difference between the sky and heaven. They had assumed that Elijah had ascended up into the sky. Therefore, they wanted the very same Elijah to come streaking across the sky in this flaming chariot, horses and all, and to descend to earth in a whirlwind. Then all he would have to do is step out of his chariot and point to the one who would be their Messiah and they would all believe. t would be just that easy. When Jesus told them that John the Baptist was the Promised Elijah, that was to come from heaven, (Matthew 11:15, 17:10-13), the Jews did not want to believe him. They did not see him come streaking across the sky in his flaming chariot and descend to earth in a whirlwind as they had been taught in their churches. They disputed, "how could this John, who was born the son of the High Priest Zechariah and his wife Elizabeth, come from Heaven?" They went to John and he told them that he was not the same person of Elijah, (not the same body or soul), but entirely a different person (John 1:21). The scriptures explain that he is of the same spirit as Elijah (a breath of the Holy Spirit, Luke 1:15-17).

These Jews were dead —Jesus considered all that did not believe in him as dead. They had not partaken of the life-giving Spirit. They wanted the same person of Elijah to come again not the one born by the Spirit of God (Luke 1:15), that had the Spirit of God from birth.

So it is today. The Christians have their eyes glued to the sky. They don't know the difference between the sky and heaven because they have not partaken of the Life-Giving Spirit. Because the scriptures state that Jesus ascended up into heaven they imagine that he ascended up into the sky, and when he returns will come streaking across the sky and the believers will ascend up into the sky to meet him. Therefore, they do not want, and are in opposition to, the Promised Ones, that descended out of heaven, sent to them by God, that were Promised in the Holy Scriptures. They are asleep in their graves (their apostate churches) — spiritually dead — and the masses won't resurrect until the thermo-nuclear bombs drop on their tombs (their churches) and opens them so they can come out. And then it may be too late for most of them.

"The Seventh Angel Sounded"

(Rev. 11:15 - SAQ pp 66)

DR. LELAND JENSEN
Knight of Baha'u'llah

"THIS STONE WITH SEVEN EYES"

This stone with seven eyes that is prophesied in the Bible (Zech. 3:9) is not only important for the recognition of the Promised Joshua, by it being the address of his appearance, but as the cross is a symbol of the perversity of the Sanhedrin Court that tried Jesus, and the corrupt judge of the Roman Pontius Pilate that acquiesced to their malicious condemnation of Him, this prison is a symbol of the gross injustices of the American legal system as well as that of the world. It shows that justice with equity is but a word in the dictionary, and the legal system but a grand facade.

The miscarriage of justice in the imprisonment of the Promised Joshua is not much dissimilar from that of ancient Joseph in the 39th chapter of Genesis, nor is it much different from St. Paul being held in prison for several years by Governor Felix with the thought in mind to extract a bribe from him (Acts 24:26,27).

Justice in America, with its legal system of lawyers is a business by which the commodity of justice is bought and sold, the price being fixed by what the traffic will bear, and by how big of a predicament they can get you into. For instance, there are no rich people in the Montana State Prison, not because the rich and affluent are not criminals, but because of their connections and that they can afford to pay the price. If you cannot or will not pay the price, you are then subjected to a biased court whose prejudices are hostile to minorities. For instance if you are a black man or a chiropractor you are most certainly guilty if you are accused. The outcome of your trial is decided ahead of time, then an act is planned by your lawyer and the county attorney, perhaps over a cup of coffee or a drink, they then proceed to the court house and put on a big show for the benefit of the jury and the public.

THIS IS THE DAY OF JUDGEMENT

The mission of Baha'u'llah is to bring about world uni and the oneness of mankind, by the establishment of Ju tice in the world. This is the long Promised Kingdom God on Earth as it is in Heaven (Luke 21:31).

The great condemnation of mankind is not just t persecution and imprisonment of God's Promised On i.e., the Bab, Baha'u'llah, and 'Abdu'l-Baha as well as Promised Joshua, but that, although they have the Boo of God in their hands they fail to recognize the Promis Ones that are prophesied to come in these Holy Boo and by so doing they cut themselves off from both t guidance of the Holy Books by which they claim to b lieve, and the guidance of the Promised Ones (Jo 5:45,46,47) and they blindly stumble into the FIRE (M thew 15:14, 23:40, Isaiah 66:15, 9:19).

The great crime of the nations is that although th have legal systems and courts of justice they have allow the thieves to steal the religions of God. The Baha'i ministration of Shoghi Effendi was usurped by the Cc enant-breaking "Hands" and perverted (bogus UHJ); though it is incorporated in the world today, this nation well as the other nations, have stood by and allowed t "Hands" to take over and illegally possess this establi ment. Therefore the "flying scroll" 20 cubits long and cubits in circumference, which is about 42 feet long a 21 feet in circumference, this being a good description the modern ballistic missile with its thermonuclear w head, is to go out over the face of the earth and enter houses of these thieves that swear falsely in the name God that, their stolen religions represent God, and dest them with a destruction that consumes both timber a stone (Zech. 5:1,2,3,4).

Dr. Leland Jensen
Knight of Baha'u'llah

www.ingramcontent.com/pod-product-compliance
Lightning Source LLC
Chambersburg PA
CBHW080217040426
42331CB00035B/3148